MARY GILMARTIN,
PATRICIA BURKE WOOD
AND CIAN O'CALLAGHAN

BORDERS, MOBILITY AND BELONGING IN THE ERA OF BREXIT AND TRUMP

POLICY PRESS SHORTS RESEARCH

First published in Great Britain in 2018 by

Policy Press
University of Bristol
1-9 Old Park Hill
Bristol
BS2 8BB
UK
t: +44 (0)117 954 5940
pp-info@bristol.ac.uk
www.policypress.co.uk

North America office:
Policy Press
c/o The University of Chicago Press
1427 East 60th Street
Chicago, IL 60637, USA
t: +1 773 702 7700
f: +1 773 702 9756
sales@press.uchicago.edu
www.press.uchicago.edu

© Policy Press 2018

British Library Cataloguing in Publication Data
A catalogue record for this book is available from the British Library.

Library of Congress Cataloging-in-Publication Data
A catalog record for this book has been requested.

ISBN 978-1-4473-4727-9 (hardback)
ISBN 978-1-4473-4729-3 (ePub)
ISBN 978-1-4473-4730-9 (Mobi)
ISBN 978-1-4473-4728-6 (ePDF)

The right of Mary Gilmartin, Patricia Burke Wood and Cian O'Callaghan to be identified as authors of this work has been asserted by them in accordance with the Copyright, Designs and Patents Act 1988.

Cover design by Policy Press
Front cover: image kindly supplied by Garrett Carr
Printed and bound in Great Britain by CPI Group (UK) Ltd, Croydon, CR0 4YY
Policy Press uses environmentally responsible print partners

Contents

List of abbreviations

CTA	Common Travel Area
DUP	Democratic Unionist Party
EU	European Union
GFA	Good Friday Agreement (also known as the Belfast Agreement)
IRA	Irish Republican Army
MAGA	Make America Great Again
NAFTA	North American Free Trade Agreement
UK	United Kingdom
UKIP	UK Independence Party
US	United States

Notes on authors

Mary Gilmartin is Professor of Geography at Maynooth University, Ireland. Her main research interests are in migration, mobilities and belonging.

Patricia Burke Wood is Professor of Geography at York University, Canada. Her main research interests include citizenship, identity and attachment to place.

Cian O'Callaghan is Assistant Professor of Geography at Trinity College Dublin, Ireland. His main research interests include creativity and place, neoliberalism, and political contestations over urban vacant spaces.

Acknowledgements

We would like to thank Emily Watt, Jamie Askew and Sarah Bird at Policy Press for their support for this book, as well as the reviewers for their helpful comments and suggestions. Thanks also to Dave Featherstone for commissioning a short article on Brexit and Ireland for *Soundings* that, in part, stimulated this project. Garrett Carr, author of *The rule of the land: Walking Ireland's border*, kindly shared border images with us. We are very grateful to him for his generosity.

ONE

Introduction

The early 21st century has witnessed a growing politicisation of migration and citizenship. This is a global phenomenon, and one with a long history. Despite assertions of an increasingly borderless and globalised world, a reversal or at least a backlash appears to be taking place. Perhaps such promises were always illusory. The neoliberal loosening of trade regulations across borders has been selective and uneven, with the movement of some goods, information, capital and people eased, while for others, it remains or has been made difficult or impossible.

The current moment is emerging as a crucial period in which the neoliberal consensus, while still strongly asserted, is nevertheless being contested through renegotiations of migration, citizenship and globalisation's promise of a borderless world. Fundamental questions of the right to move and the right to stay, the right to belong, and the right to contest the status quo are in flux. Two watershed moments stand out. On 23 June 2016, the UK voted to leave the European Union (EU). The vote in favour of 'Brexit' marked the first time that a country had chosen to leave the EU since the 1957 Treaty of Rome, which set up the European Economic Community. Just over four months later, on 8 November 2016, the US elected

Donald Trump as its president. A political outsider who had never previously held office, Trump vowed to 'Make America Great Again'. His campaign pledge both targeted the efforts of the previous president, Barack Obama, and harkened back to a previous golden era when America was great. The Brexit vote in the UK to leave the EU and the election of Donald Trump in the US are decisions specific to their countries, but they have strong ripple effects on other countries. They are also indicative of larger political changes taking place around the world, particularly with respect to migration and citizenship policies, which have become both more liberal and more exclusive at the same time. This book explores these changes, connecting them and putting them into context at multiple scales. Through this analysis, a clearer picture of the roots of these politics emerges, as well as of the consequences for mobility, political participation and belonging in the 21st century.

Despite the claims of the Brexit and Trump campaigns, there is no golden age of mobility and secure citizenship. Much change, both positive and negative, is incremental. Bureaucracy may play as significant a role as law in determining access in practice. Nevertheless, there are tectonic political shifts that move rights and freedoms dramatically in one direction or another. Brexit and Trump appear to represent such a shift. Although separate events, the Brexit referendum and the election of Trump have also had combined effects and are part of a singular phenomenon as a trend towards isolationism, protectionism, exclusionary nationalism and possibly fascism. This trend extends beyond the UK and the US, but its occurrence in these countries has special significance and impact as they are major economies, world-leading military and diplomatic powers, major producers of globally consumed cultural products and academic scholarship, and models of Western democracy. The performance of closeness and greatness was evident when Prime Minister Theresa May became the first foreign leader to visit the White House following the inauguration of President Trump. At that meeting, Prime Minister May commented on 'the special relationship that exists between our two countries, a relationship based on the bonds of history, of family, kinship and common interests', while President Trump described that relationship as 'one of the great forces in history for justice and for peace' (The White House, 2017c). In this book, we aim to provide a critical account of this contemporary political moment in the US and the UK through a focus on migration and citizenship, set comparatively in their regional contexts. Understanding current policies and practices in the US and the UK regarding migration and citizenship is a window into larger ideas about fundamental, even existential, rights to belong and inhabit, and the ways in which individual lives become entangled in political economics and geopolitics at scales beyond their immediate reach.

Questions of migration and citizenship are at the heart of contemporary political debates in the US and the UK, and, by extension, globally. These debates are informed by the rise of new forms of right-wing populism following the 2008 global financial crisis. Since the beginning of the global financial crisis, a virulent trend of anti-globalisation from both the Left and the Right has re-emerged across Europe and North America. Left-wing anti-globalisation movements highlight the effects of neoliberal economic policies and the growing influence of transnational corporations. They argue that neoliberalism facilitates the untrammelled growth of transnational corporations, the market-led provision of public services and erosion of welfare, and the individualisation of risk. The consequences, for ordinary people, are often catastrophic. As a consequence, left-wing anti-globalisation protestors emphasise the need for greater control over transnational corporations, particularly in how they exploit national borders. In contrast, right-wing anti-globalisation protesters, while also acutely aware of the negative consequences for individuals, are more likely to seek to close borders in order to shore up the privileges of supposedly beleaguered ethnic national populations against an assumed 'influx' of migrants from poorer parts of the world. Denis MacShane (2017), formerly of Tony Blair's government, argues that Brexit is evidence that globalisation as an idea and ideal has peaked, and is rapidly being challenged by rising populist, isolationist and even xenophobic political movements across Europe. Both left-wing and right-wing movements frame the current moment as a period of broader economic and political malaise. This malaise is most often described as 'economic anxiety', particularly as experienced by the so-called white working classes in both the UK and the US. Globalisation and the border-crossing activities of transnational corporations had resulted in deindustrialisation and the outsourcing of manufacturing activity. This, in turn, undermined the traditional economic base of many communities as stable blue-collar jobs were replaced, if at all, by precarious service industry employment. In both the UK and the US, early impressions were that working-class voters had been central to the success of the winning campaigns. Closer analysis revealed such conclusions to be inaccurate, and emphasised the role of middle-class, male and white voters.

It remains, however, that both the Republican and Democratic parties, as well as the Conservative and (New) Labour parties, had left a significant portion of the countries' populations unrepresented. New nationalist and protectionist electoral politics, in some instances, filled the gap. Rogers Brubaker (2017) observes that despite recent defeats of parties of the Far Right, populist parties, both Left and Right, continue to enjoy support across Europe. He argues that even those who have positioned themselves as against populism engage in populism themselves, attempting to mobilise people around vague ideas of resistance. As an example, En Marche!, founded by Emmanuel Macron in France in 2016, was explicitly described as 'a movement, not a party'. Through En Marche!, Macron appealed 'directly to "the people" beyond divisions of left and right and [promised] to "re-found" the political system' (Brubaker,

2017). Macron, like Trump, traded on being an outsider, even though both men were paradoxically at the centre of powerful political, economic or cultural networks. Macron and Trump also highlight the way in which the political spectrum has shifted to the Right, since Macron was previously a member of the Socialist Party in France, while Trump was previously a registered Democrat. As Brubaker (2017) points out, even social-democratic parties embraced neoliberal policies. However, in the context of contemporary Europe, he argues that a 'perfect storm' of economic, migration and security crises has enabled the Right, in particular, to narrate a Europe in crisis, with insecure borders and a lack of unity and solidarity. This is exacerbated by challenges to previously acknowledged authorities and experts. In the case of Brexit, all major political and economic leaders within and outside the UK advised a vote against leaving the EU, while Trump's election campaign in the US was also a refusal of experts, of political experience, of diplomacy and compromise, and of assertions of basic competence.

In this book, we use our shared and extensive experience as migration and citizenship researchers to show the striking similarities in these contemporary political debates, and to consider the implications of these debates for how migration and citizenship is understood, experienced and policed. We do this by addressing three key issues that are central to the current politicisation of migration and citizenship, but that take particular forms in the UK and the US. These three issues, each of which is discussed in a separate chapter, are borders and walls, mobility, and belonging. Borders and walls are the material articulation of state boundaries and state sovereignty. In the Trump election campaign, and in the arguments by those in favour of Brexit, the idea of taking back control of 'our' borders was a common refrain. Both focused on the role of the border as a bulwark against immigration. Political discourses about controlling borders served as a synonym for imposing greater restrictions on the numbers of immigrants legally permitted to enter the UK and the US. For Trump, border control referred to the land border between the US and Mexico. One of his campaign promises was to extend and enlarge the physical wall between the two countries, the building of which began under the Clinton presidency in the early 1990s. Trump wanted a 'physically imposing' barrier between the US and Mexico as a way of stemming illegal immigration. In contrast, this was not a priority for the UK, despite the fact that many of its EU partners were reinforcing their physical borders. That Britain is an island, with only a rail-tunnel link to France, may well explain this lack of attention. However, this conveniently ignores the land border between Northern Ireland and the Republic of Ireland,[1] which, following Brexit, will become an external EU border. We discuss the implications of 'hard' and 'soft borders', as well as the politics of bordering, in Chapter Two.

In the contemporary political moment, the relationship between borders and mobility is clear. The role of borders is increasingly seen as the regulation of the movement of people: facilitating easy movement across borders for some, but making that movement more difficult for most. In contrast, the mobility of capital, through the actions of transnational corporations in particular, receives little attention. In Chapter Three, we focus on the mobility of people and show how this has been politicised by both the Trump presidency and the Brexit vote and its aftermath. We focus on two different types of mobility: short-term travel and longer-term migration. First, we discuss the travel ban that was signed by President Trump on 27 January 2017, the same day he welcomed the UK prime minister to the White House. Second, we discuss the way in which migration was framed as a problem by advocates of Brexit. We argue that both the travel ban and the migration problem operate in similar ways by creating hierarchies of acceptability based on nationality, race, religion or other social characteristics. This practice, we show, has historical antecedents in its articulation and enforcement of the biopolitics of mobility.

The emphasis on borders and mobility has, at its core, the question of belonging. Those who are deemed to belong – whether belonging is framed in social or spatial terms – are permitted to be mobile and to cross borders. The issue is more fraught for those whose right to belong is questioned, in doubt or denied. We discuss the issue of belonging in Chapter Four. We first focus on citizenship, which is often described as formal belonging. While citizenship is regularly framed as 'natural' and 'common sense', our argument is that it is never fully stable or secure. We show this in practice through the example of the UK and Ireland, specifically, how the vote to leave the EU has had knock-on consequences for how citizenship and belonging is being re-imagined in both places. We contrast this with the practice of citizenship in the US, where, despite effusive expressions of unity, articulations of belonging have a deep history of division and exclusion. In this, we consider both the barriers to formal belonging experienced by undocumented residents of the US and the ways in which citizens themselves struggle to achieve inclusion and equality in the face of increasingly explicit intolerance.

Through these three substantive chapters, we show how questions around migration and citizenship are central to the current political moment. The US under Trump, and the Brexit vote in the UK, offer compelling examples of how we might consider these questions, as well as the broader political issues that they reveal. The practices we discuss are not new, and they are not unique to the US and the UK. There are, as we demonstrate, obvious historical and geographical continuities. However, the virulent nature of the debates over borders, mobility and belonging in the contemporary US and UK require our urgent attention as we seek an alternative understanding of migration and citizenship for the 21st century.

Note

1. In the book, we generally use the term 'Ireland' to refer to the Republic of Ireland. We use the term Republic of Ireland when we seek to distinguish it from Northern Ireland.

TWO

Borders and walls

Introduction

On 22 August 2017, Leo Varadkar, the newly elected Taoiseach (Prime Minister) of Ireland, paid a visit to the US–Canada border. Varadkar was wrapping up his official tour of Canada, where he had sought to closely align himself with Canadian Prime Minister Justin Trudeau. The two leaders were photographed together at state functions, diplomatic trade talks and marching in the Montreal Pride Parade, where they smiled and waved at the crowds in matching button-down shirts and chino combos. While the Canadian tour was intended to consolidate the beautiful friendship that began with a short visit by Trudeau to Dublin the previous month, Varadkar was also on a 'fact-finding' mission in light of the potential changes to Ireland's land border as a result of Brexit. With Brexit, the land border between Northern Ireland and the Republic of Ireland will become a European Union (EU) external border, and thus the soft border that currently exists could be radically revised: 'I have heard some people who are promoters of Brexit using [the US–Canada border] as an example of a solution that could work in Ireland', Varadkar was quoted as saying, 'I have heard them describe it as a soft border, I wonder if that is the case?' (Kelly, 2017). Speaking the following day from the border, he was less equivocal, saying: 'make no mistake, it's a hard border' (Anderson, 2017).

For the last three decades, pro-globalisation advocates have been flaunting the promise of a 'borderless world' (Friedman, 2006), but practices of bordering have become more complex and uneven (Jones, 2016). While for some groups of people, movement has become frictionless, for others, the right to move has been restricted as borders have been militarised (Jones and Johnson, 2016). In the current context of Brexit and the Trump presidency, the performance of borders, if not the actual practice, is being significantly transformed so that borders are invoked and materially enforced in new ways. However, the intrinsically interconnected nature of the global economy has also meant that the impact of transformations in the UK and the US are having ramifications beyond the territories that they immediately bound. In this chapter, we are interested in how the dominant performance of borders and bordering is being reworked through Brexit and the Trump presidency. The impact of Brexit has brought renewed attention and anxiety to the 310-mile land border between the Republic of Ireland and Northern Ireland, while also unsettling the norms around the EU's external borders. A key feature of the Leave campaign played off nationalist and xenophobic discourses of the once-great Britain 'taking back control' of national borders. In the US, President Donald Trump campaigned on the promise to 'build a wall' between Mexico and the US and, not incidentally, to 'make Mexico pay for it'. Since his election, the US–Mexico border has been intensely politicised and racialised. We contrast this with the relative lack of anxiety regarding the US–Canada border. Through an analysis of these performances, we consider the ways in which borders are discursively invoked and materially reconfigured such that particular types of migrants are constructed as a threat and specific borders in need of securitisation.

The rise of walls in a 'borderless world'

The recent story of international borders is one of extreme ambivalence. For the past 20 years, the dominant narrative has been about the removal of borders in a globalised world. Yet, as the geographer Reece Jones (2016: 4) notes, an estimated 40,000 people died crossing a border in 2014 and 2015. How is it the case that borders are simultaneously disappearing and becoming ever-more deadly places? In reality, borders are of key importance to the functioning of global society. This has entailed a set of dual processes. While some borders are becoming invisible, other borders have been securitised by an increased military and police presence and by the erection of walls and fences. Similarly, while movement across borders has become frictionless for some, for others, it has been heavily restricted. This contradiction is most readily expressed by the EU. From 1995, the Schengen Agreement has created visa-free movement through the internal borders of Europe, which, by 2014, included 26 participating countries. While these changes seemed to confer the possibility of a borderless world, the reality was that EU borders were 'simply moved [to] ... the external boundaries of the European Union at the Mediterranean and on its eastern edges' (Jones, 2016: 16). Frontex, the agency established by the EU in 2004 to manage the operational coordination at its external borders, has been central to the creation of what critics have labelled 'Fortress Europe', in reference to the system of border patrols and migrant detention centres that have been developed to prevent 'illegal migration' into Europe. The various actions of the agency contribute to the normalisation of the securitisation of borders, while as a set of discursive practices, the agency's operations construct the idea of the EU as a 'bordered territory' (Léonard, 2010).

Borders are 'sovereign sites of security as well as mobile places of encounter' (Till et al, 2013: 52). Borders serve to demarcate the boundaries of state territory and communicate who is included and excluded. However, bordering practices are applied in uneven and inconsistent ways, and, as such, borders are experienced subjectively by those who seek to cross them. This is most readily expressed in the hardening of EU external borders in response to the recent migrant crisis – in the form of a razor-wire fence along Hungary's border with Serbia, the offshoring of border patrols to the Mediterranean Sea and the EU's outsourcing of migrant detention to Libya and Morocco (Jones, 2016; Minca and Rijke, 2017). Migrants seeking refuge from war, conflict or poverty are enduring increasingly dangerous crossings, and are perceived as a threat to the stability of the states that they are hoping to enter. Within this context, bordering practices produce a discourse of Othering that reinforces a hierarchy of mobility.

One outcome of the heightened attention to borders has been a dramatic increase in the announcing and building of walls (Minca and Rijke, 2017). This trend has been broadly explained in two different ways. One view, epitomised by Wendy Brown (2010), argues that militarised borders are a sign of waning state power, rather than a show of strength. Another perspective, spearheaded, in part, by Judith Butler's (2006, 2016) work, views 'the new border security projects ... as part of a broader trend by sovereign states, their agents and their intermediaries that re-articulates sovereign authority at borders and within state territories' (Jones, 2016: 194; see also Till et al, 2013). From these perspectives, states are either losing control of borders in the face of immutable globalisation and erecting barricades to reassert their authority, or, alternatively, extending their reach through the biopolitical 'management of populations' rather than territory, with borderlands one particularly dense zone of control (Coleman, 2007, 2012). This contradiction speaks more broadly to how borders have been configured within the political landscape of the last few decades.

Various writers have described the emergence of a 'post-democratic' consensus in the years following the fall of the Berlin Wall and the decline of state socialism (for different perspectives, see Rancière, 1999; Crouch, 2004; Fukuyama, 2006). A common feature of these arguments is that the combination of liberal democracy and neoliberal capitalism has become the dominant state model for much of the world. One outcome of the relative stability of this consensus has been the formation of a set of international norms around borders. Legal and technical arrangements – such as the Schengen Agreement or the North American Free Trade Agreement (NAFTA) between the US, Canada and Mexico – have regularised the movement of (certain) people and goods across (certain) borders. Concurrently, states have restricted the movement of others. These restrictions have been rationalised through discourses on security, which construct the need for states to protect themselves against the 'threat' of 'dangerous' migrants. As Isabell Lorey (2015) has argued, in the post-9/11 context, this has been articulated both as a threat from terrorism and as a threat to the economic security of privileged nations. Importantly, discursive work is involved in producing narratives about such perceived threat. Elizabeth Povinelli (2011: 25) has suggested that 'late liberal' societies[1] have had to straddle the need to promote neoliberal market values while also presenting their actions as 'humanitarian', even when they have 'lethal' consequences. Government actions in relation to events like the migrant and refugee crisis are presented as the 'humane', altruistic and sensible response of progressive world leaders, Povinelli argues, despite resulting in the deaths of thousands and the internment of thousands more (Povinelli, 2011; see also Darling, 2009).

The 'late liberal' era has thus produced norms about how world borders are performed. This performance is often 'quiet' in nature, involving the creation of more restrictive migration policies with little fanfare while promoting the idea of disappearing borders. However, recent events have indicated a different, more overt, performance of the border – akin to what Minca and Rijke (2017) have termed 'wall announcing' and 'wall building'. Trump's 'announcing' of his intention to build a wall along the US–Mexico border or the prominent mantra of 'taking back our borders' as part of the Leave campaign in the Brexit referendum signal a transformation of the dominant performance of borders in the political sphere. The appeal and popularity of these overt border performances can, in part, be explained by the collapse of the political consensus in the aftermath of the global financial crisis, which has brought about new forms of anti-globalisation. Within this context, the promise of a 'return' to state-controlled borders has populist appeal. However, the political earthquake that these events have precipitated has also disrupted the global alignment of borders in more fundamental ways and unsettled taken-for-granted spatial relationships. In this chapter, we use the examples of recent debates about the borders between Northern Ireland and the Republic of Ireland, and the US and Mexico, to explore these shifts.

Brexit, Northern Ireland and the borders of Europe

In the UK, 'the border' has been receiving new policy attention since 2007:

> Since then, the term has appeared in a series of legislative acts addressing migration control, notably in the Borders, Citizenship and Immigration Act 2009. Also, one of the top three policy promises of the party manifestos published during the run-up of the 2015 General Elections in the UK referred to stricter controls by strengthening the UK border. (Vollmer, 2017: 296)

The new awareness of 'the border' in public debate in the UK showcases the difference that often exists between the practice and performance of borders. In an analysis of discourses about the UK border in relation to migration, Bastian Vollmer found that there was a stark difference between policy and public newspaper representations. While the former focused on *security* concerns relating to the EU's 'open borders', the latter framed open borders in terms of *insecurity*, the 'threat' resulting from 'open borders and globalisation gone wild' (Vollmer, 2017: 305–6). Thus, while both focused on security-related issues, policy debates were framed in terms of managing borders while public debates were characterised by 'evoking fear', as well as a demand that the British government 'fix the problem of open borders' (Vollmer, 2017: 306).

The growing securitisation of the border between France and the UK located around the ferry ports at Calais offers an illustration. Calais gained worldwide media attention as the migrant crisis escalated during 2015 and 2016, when it became synonymous with a large-scale refugee camp, the 'Jungle'.[2] During the period leading up to, and indeed following, the demolition of the camp in October 2016, Calais was subject to considerable UK state intervention in border security. As detailed by Oli Mould (2017: 391–2), as Home Secretary, Theresa May and her French counterpart, Bernard Cazeneuve, signed a cooperation agreement 'that saw £15 million of funds from the UK being diverted to strengthen the police presence in Calais around the refugee camps, as well as to build more fences and walls around the ferry and rail terminals'. In March 2016, David Cameron pledged an additional £17 million, and the UK government later advertised an £80 million contract for a private security firm to conduct 'operational activities' in the ports of Calais, Dunkirk and Coquelles. Nevertheless, media coverage in the UK often represented the Calais border crossing as a threat. For example, in October 2016, several tabloid newspapers carried photographs of child refugees arriving in the

UK from Calais, questioning their age and implying that they could potentially be Islamic terrorists exploiting 'open borders' to enter the UK (Bowden, 2016).

These types of fears were significantly stoked, consolidated and conflated by the Brexit referendum. The slogan 'let's take back control of our country', popularised by the UK Independence Party (UKIP), became central to the Leave campaign. UKIP published a series of propagandistic campaign posters attacking the EU's 'open border' policy. One such poster, depicting an escalator running from a beach up a cliff to an English-looking landscape, had the tagline: 'No borders, No control'. While UKIP sometimes referenced migrants from within the EU, pro-Brexit media often conflated the issue with migrants attempting to smuggle themselves into Britain from other parts of the world. The *Daily Mail*, for example, published a picture of police discovering migrants from Iraq and Kuwait being smuggled into the UK in a truck with the headline: 'We're from Europe – Let us in!' (see Allegretti, 2016). These discourses selectively played on the EU rhetoric of 'open borders' while ignoring the increased militarisation of the external border. As commentators noted, while the pro-Brexit side drew heavily on 'the border' as 'a key discursive icon and manifestation of controlling migration' (Vollmer, 2017: 296), debates showed very little awareness of what the implications of 'taking back control' might actually be (Chu, 2017). Within this context, the Northern Ireland border provides a fascinating example of the complexity of borders and the impact of Brexit.

Throughout the Brexit campaign, debates concerning the perceived threat of 'uncontrolled migration' tacitly focused on the UK mainland, with attention given to Calais, for example. However, the UK's only land border, between Northern Ireland and the Republic of Ireland, was conspicuous by its absence. One of the most prominent material impacts of the Good Friday Agreement signed by the British and Irish governments on 10 April 1998 was the removal of the hard border between the north and south of the island, along with the dismantling of border posts and checkpoints. During the period of the Troubles – the name given to the period of sectarian violence between 1968 and 1998, which was mostly confined to Northern Ireland but, at times, also affected the UK and the Republic of Ireland – border crossings were heavily militarised and consequently became frequent targets for Irish Republican Army (IRA) attacks. The largely invisible border that has been in operation since 1998 is threatened by Brexit.

Before the referendum, Sinn Féin's Martin McGuinness suggested that the implications of Brexit for Northern Ireland would be 'absolutely enormous': 'Our land border with the Republic could be a major issue, given the desire in Europe to tighten borders' (*Irish Independent*, 2016). Similarly, former UK Prime Ministers Tony Blair and John Major, in a joint speech, warned that a Leave vote could undermine the 'carefully constructed foundations' of Peace in Northern Ireland (Cooper, 2016b). Commentators referenced the '£2.5bn [Northern Ireland received] in the last EU funding round, and a further £2bn is promised before 2020' (Gaw, 2016), along with the potential economic impacts of the return of a hard border. Running through these debates were concerns that the equilibrium achieved through the peace process would be derailed by a 'hard Brexit':

> [G]iven the emphasis on immigration during the referendum debates, border controls are likely to become a priority in the event of a Brexit vote.... To install physical checkpoints along the border would instantly undermine a hard-won peace, and the psychological impact alone would be catastrophic. A return of those barricaded towers and armed checkpoints will stir up emotional memories for many Northern Irish people who witnessed years of violence in border towns such as Newry, Omagh and

Derry, and there is a very real fear that they may lead to a resurgence of dissident activity. (Gaw, 2016)

Brexit supporters dismissed such concerns as disingenuous. The British Prime Minister, Theresa May, and Secretary of State for Northern Ireland, Theresa Villiers, suggested that the Common Travel Area (CTA), which has existed in some form since 1922, when the Irish Free State was established, and allows free movement of citizens between the two states (Ryan, 2016), would override EU border policy and ensure that there would be no return to a hard border. After Labour Party MP and former Secretary of State for Northern Ireland Peter Mandelson commented that Brexit could set back the peace process, the DUP MP for East Antrim, Sammy Wilson, more colourfully suggested that the comments were 'not just spin, they would be credit to the most energetic acrobat', adding that 'the open border at present does not cause problems of large scale illegal immigration' (Cooper, 2016a). The Northern Irish border, in this sense, was constructed by Brexit supporters as a stand-alone issue separate from the problems posed by the EU in relation to 'open borders' and 'illegal immigration'. Contrastingly, those opposed to Brexit situated the Northern Irish border within a wider constellation of EU borders, noting that its functionality was being rendered precarious by a potential Leave vote.

Following the referendum result on 23 June 2016, contentious debates were set in motion about the complex situation of the Northern Ireland border and the implications that this would have for the island of Ireland, the UK and the EU. The return to a hard border seemed an impossibility within the context of the peace process, while within the context of EU border policy, it seemed an impossibility that the border would stay as it was. While the UK and Ireland opted out of Schengen from the start, the CTA made an open border policy possible. Given trends towards increased militarisation of borders elsewhere in Europe, along with pressures to limit future immigration and restrict the rights of immigrants in the UK, there would surely be pressure to securitise a new EU external border. Various technological and technocratic solutions were floated, including the possibility of electronic borders being introduced, as well as a proposal by the UK government to push Britain's immigration controls back to Irish ports and airports such that individuals entering Ireland could be subject to British immigration controls (Kelpie, 2016; Zeffman and Rogan, 2016). By the end of 2016, however, numerous proposed solutions were ruled unworkable and key stakeholders began talking in terms of the 'unique situation' of Northern Ireland. In January 2017, the EU's chief Brexit negotiator, Michel Barnier, spoke of the imperative to retain the soft border (O'Brien, 2017).

In August 2017, the UK government published a position paper that sought to 'address the unique circumstances of Northern Ireland and the Republic of Ireland in light of the UK's withdrawal from, and new partnership with, the European Union (EU)' (HM Government, 2017). The position paper identified 'four broad areas' for specific focus: upholding the Belfast ('Good Friday') Agreement in all its parts; maintaining the CTA and associated rights; avoiding a hard border for the movement of goods; and aiming to preserve North–South and East–West cooperation, including on energy (HM Government, 2017). The paper suggested that the 'high-level objectives' of the UK government, Irish government and the EU were 'wholly aligned' with regard to the four broad areas. However, the document offered little detail of how these objectives would be achieved. In the North, Sinn Féin called the UK proposals 'delusional' (Moriarty, 2017). This was reflective of the paradoxical position that was beginning to characterise the UK's stance on negotiations: the ideal outcome was to retain the status quo of the current situation, while the promise of Brexit was to fundamentally change existing arrangements.

The EU exploited the border issue to pressure the UK government to make favourable concessions during the first round of negotiations before the substantive economic and trade issues would be addressed. A paper by the EU Brexit Task Force leaked to selected media in November 2017 suggested 'that the only way to avoid a hard border would be for the rules on both sides of the border to remain the same when it came to the EU single market and customs union' (Connelly, 2018). Furthermore, media discussions also implied that Ireland could use its veto as an EU27 member state to block the negotiations moving to stage two. The Irish government capitalised on these developments to position itself centrally within the negotiations (O'Toole, 2017). A compromise was reached and, on 15 December 2017, the EU27 formally granted permission to proceed to the second stage of negotiations. The text of the final deal reads:

> The United Kingdom remains committed to protecting North–South cooperation and to its guarantee of avoiding a hard border. Any future arrangements must be compatible with these overarching requirements. The United Kingdom's intention is to achieve these objectives through the overall EU–UK relationship. Should this not be possible, the United Kingdom will propose specific solutions to address the unique circumstances of the island of Ireland. (Transcript from Murray, 2018)

On 28 February 2018, the EU released draft text for the Withdrawal Agreement, including specific language for the Irish border. It proposes to maintain an open border, despite the UK's exit from both the single market and the customs union, through complete alignment of all relevant policy. The draft agreement states: 'The territory of Northern Ireland, excluding the territorial waters of the United Kingdom (the "territory of Northern Ireland"), shall be considered to be part of the customs territory of the Union' (European Commission, 2018: 101). The UK commitment to having no hard border was reiterated in Prime Minister May's speech on 2 March 2018, though she also insisted that the common market of the UK would be maintained (Sparrow, 2018).

Both the centrality of the border to negotiations and the lack of a definitive resolution of the issue in the first round suggest how revising the border unsettles the dominant performance and practice of borders within the EU in three key ways. First, it reveals this unsettling in the disruption that a hard border would bring to economic trade between the Republic of Ireland, Northern Ireland and the UK. Much discussion was focused on the already economically precarious regions along both sides of the border. The results of the 2016 Irish Census revealed that the number of people commuting across the border for work was 7,037 in 2016, up from 6,419 in 2011, while the number of students was 2,299, down from 3,117 in 2011 (Central Statistics Office, 2017a). The numbers travelling for consumption or leisure are much higher. Media discussions suggested that people in 'Donegal and Derry can easily cross the Border two or more times every day' (McDonnell, 2016), and that the return of border checks would be hugely detrimental. The impact of the border on international trade was also a feature: 'Britain is Ireland's largest trading partner and two-way trade between the two countries stands at about £1bn a week, with an equal trading balance in imports and exports' (O'Carroll, 2016). Likewise, in 2015, Northern Ireland sent £10.7 billion of goods to Britain; over the same period, the Republic of Ireland was Northern Ireland's biggest external trading partner, with £2.7 billion in goods exported (HM Government, 2017). Should customs checks be reintroduced with the change to an external EU border, the impact on business in all three jurisdictions could be extensive.

Second, Brexit unsettles borders through the re-emergence of unresolved postcolonial legacies in Ireland. The Irish government has called the soft border 'the most tangible symbol of the peace process' (Irish Government, 2017). The 'hard border' is invoked as a spectre of the Troubles, a warning of the prospect of returning to the violent borders of the past. The UK government's position paper spells this out explicitly:

> In 1972 there was a chain of 17 HM Customs and Excise boundary posts at the major road crossing points along the Northern Ireland land border, with the other (over 200) crossings not approved for vehicular traffic. During the 'Troubles', customs posts were frequently the subject of bombing attacks. Border crossings and checkpoints were manned by a very substantial military and security presence, including a series of 'watchtowers' in border areas, and a number of border roads were blocked by the security forces adding to the disruption created by the approved road network.... All military security installations and other infrastructure were removed following the [Good Friday] Agreement and the border today is invisible and seamless across its 310 mile/500 km length. (HM Government, 2017)

The transition from a hard 'violent' border to a soft border is thus presented as a narrative of civilising progress. The disappearance of the material border has given the appearance of a lack of division on the island of Ireland. The UK government's position paper suggests that the relationship between Ireland and the UK 'has never been better or more settled than today', and references the official visit of the Queen to Ireland in 2011 as evidence of a 'modern partnership'. However, as noted by O'Callaghan (2011), within the postcolonial context, the success of such visits is dependent on a negotiated 'remembering and forgetting' of the shared history between the two nations. This 'modern partnership' has been enabled through much border work, in the form of the CTA and other agreements, but is also facilitated by the supposed equality between the two states as members of the EU. This presumption of equality was challenged during the first round of Brexit negotiations. In an editorial, for instance, *The Sun* suggested that the 'naïve, young' Taoiseach Leo Varadkar should 'shut his gob' on Brexit. When Channel 4 asked members of the public in a vox pop to draw the border between the north and the south of the island of Ireland, the results were decidedly mixed, with one attempt cleaving the island in half with a border stretching from Galway in the West to Dublin in the East. While some of those interviewed noted the complexity of the border situation in the context of Brexit, one man suggested that it would be 'in everyone's interest' for Ireland to leave the EU along with the UK, while another woman opined that 'the Irish are just making trouble because they lost' (see Murray, 2017). These and other political statements served to reinforce the extent to which lingering postcolonial attitudes were evident in sections of British public discourse.

Third, Brexit unsettles, and potentially reshapes, the geography of the EU external border by potentially creating a new external EU border in an awkward position. Symbolically, EU border policy has been based on a clear demarcation of 'inside' and 'outside'. The hardening of the external border has been justified on the basis of the 'responsibility' of individual member states to each other and to the shared project of European integration. In recent years, the series of contentious exchanges between the EU and countries like Hungary and Bulgaria over their treatment of refugees has shown the delicate balancing act of late-liberal governance already coming under strain. The various challenges posed by the Northern Irish border offer another example – the reinstating of a hard border would explicitly go against the project of European integration by negatively impacting a member state, Ireland, seen as a casualty of the UK's decision to leave the union. We can see this in the central role accorded to Ireland during the first round of negotiations. In recognising the special status of the Northern Irish border, the EU highlights its inconsistent application of border security. In an address to the Oireachtas – both Irish houses of parliament – in May 2017,

Michel Barnier suggested that 'European integration helped to remove borders that once existed on maps and in minds. Brexit changes the external borders of the EU. I will work with you to avoid a hard border' (McMurry, 2017). This perspective was reinforced by President of the European Council Donald Tusk, who, following a meeting with Taoiseach Varadkar in December 2017, stated: 'if the UK offer is unacceptable for Ireland, it will also be unacceptable for the EU' (quoted in Connelly, 2018). This clearly separates the Irish as 'insiders', whereas similar special considerations are not made for other external borders.

The negotiations also demonstrate how hegemonic the EU has become in shaping norms around borders. The UK position paper goes to lengths to perform the legitimacy of the CTA, invoking its longevity and importance to the Good Friday Agreement, as well as how bilateral agreements between Ireland and the UK have involved a 'joint programme of work in support of securing the external CTA border' (HM Government, 2017). The CTA was used to perform the legitimacy of border agreements outside the EU programme, noting that 'the intermingling of rights can make it difficult to distinguish what rights accrue under the CTA as opposed to other EU instruments' (HM Government, 2017). Interestingly, as part of media discussion about Northern Ireland's border, the role of former US President Bill Clinton in the peace process has been highlighted (Roszman, 2017). The associations made between the UK, the US and, by extension, Ireland demonstrate the geopolitical importance of Brexit. The ripple effects of border realignments in the UK and the US are likely to be extensive and, as the case of Northern Ireland suggests, unsettle the norms of borders more fundamentally.

Great walls, entangled lives and bordering America

Immediately following the announcement of his candidacy for president in June 2015, Donald Trump declared his intention to build a border wall between the US and Mexico:

> I will build a great wall — and nobody builds walls better than me, believe me — and I'll build them very inexpensively. I will build a great, great wall on our southern border, and I will make Mexico pay for that wall. Mark my words. (Donald Trump, June 2015, cited in Minca and Rijke, 2017)

The border wall featured prominently throughout the campaign. In July 2016, the Republican platform for the election included a reference to the 'border wall [that] must cover the entirety of the southern border and must be sufficient to stop both vehicular and pedestrian traffic' (Countable, no date). While many expected the colourful piece of rhetoric to be dropped following the election, as was the case with the 'travel ban' discussed in Chapter Three, President Trump immediately doubled-down on his promise. On 25 January 2017, he issued an executive order entitled 'Border security and immigration enforcement improvements', which declared the intention of his administration to 'take all appropriate steps to immediately plan, design, and construct a physical wall along the southern border' (The White House, 2017a). Mexican President Enrique Pena Nieto condemned the decision and made it clear that Mexico would not pay for the wall. Over the following months, Trump floated budgets and blueprints for the project, suggested the imposition of a 20% import tax on Mexican goods to help pay for the construction costs, and continued his public relations offensive, extolling the benefits of his 'great wall' as 'a very effective weapon against drugs and crime' (Countable, no date). In October 2017, border wall prototypes were displayed in San

Diego as the first tangible evidence of the campaign promise (Somerville, 2017), and in February 2018, it was announced that the administration's budget plan would include US$3 billion in funding for the project (Crutsinger, 2018). Overall, Trump is seeking US$18–20 billion in funding over a 10-year period. Estimates of the cost of building a wall along the entire 2,000-mile border put it at US$67 billion, not including the cost of land acquisition. However, Trump's revised plans 'now call for a more modest, 722-mile barrier that is a mix of wall and fencing, mostly updating what's been in place for decades, while relying on drones and other methods to secure the rest' (Bloomberg, 2018). Despite these developments, the details of how (and, indeed, if) the border wall will be delivered remain unclear at the time of writing. Nevertheless, the issue has remained central to Trump's policy rhetoric.

Trump's performance of bordering is representative of recent trends in right-wing populism that invoke the threat of 'bad mobilities' (Jones and Johnson, 2016) in order to reassert national sovereignty. As Jones and Johnson (2016: 195) suggest, within the context of neoliberal globalisation, 'states are no longer content to take the "bad with the good", but rather are deluded into thinking it is possible to choose perfectly between good and bad mobilities'. In this context, 'security threats' are often invoked to protect economic privilege by limiting mobility (Lorey, 2015). Such shifts are part of the wider trend towards militarised borders discussed earlier, and, indeed, were taking place long before Trump gained office. As Jones (2016: 37) notes: 'more people have been deported from the United States during the Obama presidency than during any previous administration'. However, while Obama's was a 'quiet' performance of borders, publicly promoting tolerance and multiculturalism while, at the same time, furthering restrictive immigration controls, Trump's performance explicitly trades on the racism inherent in hierarchies of mobility. Trump's former chief strategist and founder of the right-wing publication *Breitbart*, Steve Bannon, has stated that combining economic nationalism with white ethnic nationalism was the basis of his campaign plan for the election (Kuttner, 2017). Like Brexit, 'the border' was a key symbol during the Trump election campaign, used to invoke both the fear of 'illegal migration' and a nostalgic return to the national primacy of the US in a prior phase of globalisation, represented by the MAGA (Make America Great Again) slogan. As noted by Minca and Rijke (2017), Trump declared that 'a nation without borders is not a nation. Beginning today, the United States of America gets back control of its borders, gets back its borders'. However, this belied the complex history of the US–Mexico border itself and the inconsistent ways in which border and immigration policy has been historically applied (Coleman, 2012). In this chapter, we compare the performance of the US–Mexico border as problematic with that of the relatively unproblematic US–Canada border.

Trump's portrayal of US territorial borders as marking a natural sovereign geographical area ignores a more entangled history. The apparent fixity of the US–Mexico and US–Canada borders is relatively new; until recently, these borders were characterised by a considerable degree of movement between the territories. Until the 20th century, more people migrated to the US from Canada than moved to Canada, including significant French populations in New England, while Americans were the majority population in 19th-century Canada. The current route of the US–Mexican border was only established in 1848 and 1853 with the signing of the treaty of Guadalupe Hidalgo and the Gadsden Purchase at the end of the Mexican–American War (Jones, 2016: 33). Thus, the borderland is hardly sacrosanct national sovereign territory of the US. There is a strong sense of belonging to the area as historically Mexican territory, as we discuss in Chapter Four. John Sayles, in his 1996 film *Lone star*, used incest as a metaphor to explore the entangled shared cultural heritage characteristic of the border (Arreola, 2005). Arreola (2010: 331) describes the US–Mexico borderland as a 'tricultural zone – Native, Hispanic, Anglo – cut by a boundary line'. Likewise, the current fervour around restricting mobility across these borders is a relatively recent phenomenon. The US did not create border controls until 1924. Initially, the border patrol focused on the Canadian border, particularly targeting Asian migrants, but it gradually shifted to the Mexican border (Jones, 2016: 33–4). However, as Coleman (2012: 403) argues, the history of US immigration and border control is more 'geographically messy'. Border concerns have shifted over time and space.

Scholarship on US immigration enforcement views a major shift as taking place in the mid-1990s (Coleman, 2012). Until the 1990s, the border force was just over 3,000 personnel and operated on the basis of a strategy of interdiction, allowing migrants to cross into the US before detaining them and releasing them back on the Mexican side (Jones, 2016: 33). From the mid-1990s, the border patrol implemented a new policy 'known as "prevention by deterrence" … [intended] to shift migrants away from urban crossings and toward more remote areas that would render the journey less appealing' (Squire, 2014: 12). Post-9/11, increased concerns about 'security threats' were used to justify a substantial increase in border patrol agents (Coleman, 2007), which numbered more than 20,000 by 2010 (Jones, 2016: 33–4). These factors led to a criminalisation of migration and a surge in deportations, increasing from about 20,000 deportations per year before 1986 to 400,000 per year by the mid-2000s, coupled with the construction of substantial border infrastructure – today, 1,070 km of the 3,169 km border are fenced (Jones, 2016: 35–7). All of this has changed the context of mobility across the US–Mexico border in physical, embodied and representational terms (see Cresswell, 2010; see also the discussion in Chapter Three). As Jones and Johnson (2016: 196) put it:

A generation ago, a trip to the US often meant a quick sprint across the border in an urban centre like El Paso-Juarez or Tijuana-San Diego. Today, the crossing involves an arduous journey through dangerous deserts or a claustrophobic ride through a checkpoint, stuffed under a seat or in a cramped shipping container.

The result is an increasingly dangerous border crossing for migrants coming from Mexico (Squire, 2014) and the expansion of border security into the wider border region (Coleman, 2007). US border patrol has 'recovered more than 6,000 bodies along the US–Mexican border since the 1990s' (Jones, 2016: 43–6) and shot and killed 33 people between 2010 and 2015. Unequal economic relationships across the border, along with cartel violence on the Mexican side, continue to push migrants into making the crossing through hostile terrain. However, in opposition to Trump's skewed version of Mexican migrants exploiting 'open borders', it is:

> widely accepted that NAFTA, the North American Free Trade Agreement has ensured the US access to an abundant supply of cheap labour south of the border ... [and] has long been the subject of criticism by Mexican activists for its devastation of the traditional Mexican rural economy. (Taylor, C., 2017)

The increasingly dangerous border crossing has also given rise to a range of activist work. In just one example, volunteers with the group 'No More Deaths' place water, food, blankets and other crucial goods in the southern Arizona borderlands along routes that are heavily travelled by undocumented migrants (Johnson, 2015: 1245).

Trump's depictions of the US–Mexico border build upon and amplify historic precedents, constructing a narrative of Mexican migrants as exploitative of the US economy and possibly dangerous criminals. When discussing migration from Mexico during his presidential announcement speech, Trump suggested that:

> When Mexico sends its people, they're not sending their best.... They're sending people that have lots of problems, and they're bringing those problems with us. They're bringing drugs. They're bringing crime. They're rapists. And some, I assume, are good people. (Lee, 2015)

Moreover, Trump suggested that the Mexican government itself was complicit in 'forcing their most unwanted people into the United States' (Lee, 2015). Activist groups have also been targeted 'in the Trump administration's crackdown on immigration advocates' (Devereaux, 2018). As of January 2018, nine members of the No More Deaths group had been charged with felony crimes and misdemeanours in relation to their work supporting migrants. Activists involved noted that the border patrol had, until recently, surveilled and permitted the activities of the group but that 'now all of the sudden it's all changed' (quoted in Devereaux, 2018). Thus, Trump's performance of the US–Mexico border has also translated into more punitive practices on the ground.

In direct contrast, the US–Canada border – which has large, open, unguarded stretches – was viewed as one of mutual benefit to both governments and not a source of 'illegal migration'. While the Trump administration has been relatively silent on the issue, in April 2017, current White House Chief of Staff John Kelly called Canada 'a friend, an ally', commended 'their law enforcement, their commitment', and suggested 'I'd like to see the northern border to be even thinner, if you will, so that the movement, safely and securely, of commerce and people can be even streamlined more'. As one caveat, he did note a 'little' recent increase in the number of Mexicans crossing illegally from Canada (Dale, 2017). Following Trump's election, there was a notable rise of refugee claimants in the US walking to the Canadian border because of the perception of danger and precarity in the US and the perception of safety in Canada: 'There were 4,345 illegal border crossings into Canada in the first six months of the year, according to federal government figures. The majority, 3,350, occurred in Quebec, followed by 646 in Manitoba and 332 in British Columbia' (*Globe and Mail*, 2017a). The dramatic photographs of families walking through the snow caught the public's attention (Taylor, A., 2017), although the inflow was not unprecedented. A report by the School of Public Policy at the University of Calgary found that the 'number of asylum claimants in Canada ebbs and flows over time and by province', with the number of claimants previously spiking in 2001 (Wilkins, 2017). Rumours circulating among refugees resident in the US that Canada was accepting refugees were inaccurate, but the perception was nevertheless aided by Canadian Prime Minister Justin Trudeau's own performance of borders in response to Trump's inauguration. In January 2017, Trudeau tweeted: 'To those fleeing persecution, terror and war, Canadians will welcome you, regardless of your faith. Diversity is our strength. #WelcomeToCanada'. While 'Mr. Trudeau and his government had no intention of welcoming *everyone* who walked across the border' (*Globe and Mail*, 2017b), his performance positioned Canada in opposition to Trump's rhetoric.

Despite John Kelly's promotion of a more 'streamlined' border between the US and Canada, however, media commentators have speculated that Trump wants to sabotage the NAFTA talks so as to make the customs border unworkable, with one non-US official describing US negotiators as 'like lawyers who hate their clients' (Panetta, 2017). Since becoming president, Trump has pursued a contradictory set of economic policies. As geographer Padraig Carmody (2017) notes, Trump's economic policy could be described in terms of 'neoliberalism in one country'. He argues that Trump:

is trying to create a new class compromise in the United States based on a retraction of its overseas commitments ... where deregulation will be further encouraged and public provision of services, such as healthcare, will be undercut domestically. He will, however, attempt to insulate the country from the impacts of the free market through economic protectionism and also try to 'keep the world outside out' through immigration restriction and enforcement. (Carmody, 2017)

Thus, while the US–Canada border is perhaps part of Trump's economic strategy, it is not depicted as a 'dangerous' border in the same way as the US–Mexico border is.

Although border control policy has shifted little from the policy under Obama, the spectre of the wall and the uneven performance of the respective borders to the south and the north has, nevertheless, begun to transform the relationships between Mexico, the US and Canada. Within the US, the border wall is part of a set of policy actions that have served to legitimise more overt displays of exclusionary nationalism, and, indeed, white supremacy. At the same time, migrants with precarious status in the US have begun to feel less secure and some have looked towards the border with Canada as a safer long-term option. This is not wholly unwarranted as Trump has initiated the 'roundup of refugees and illegal immigrants living anywhere in the country – and not just near the Mexican border, as was the policy under the previous administration – and their transfer to far-flung detention centres' (*Globe and Mail*, 2017a). However, although Trudeau has positioned Canada as the antithesis of Trump's America in terms of border control, Canadian immigration policy – while less restrictive than the US – still operates on the basis of a regime that attempts to sort between good and bad mobilities. As we discuss in Chapter Four, Trump's construction of the US–Mexico border as a threat and his overt performance of exclusionary bordering has contributed to the unravelling of already-frayed feelings of belonging in the US context. However, despite Trump's clampdown, activists at the US–Mexico border have continued to pursue strategies that imagine the border in a different way. On the morning of Trump's inauguration, 50 women from the Boundless Across Borders group hailing from both sides of the border joined 'one another at the El Paso international bridge for braiding borders in response to the dangerous rhetoric of the recent election' (González, 2017). Standing in pairs and back to back, the women braided their hair or scarves together in a silent protest emphasising their solidarity and the shared lives they live across the entangled border. Furthermore, artist Enrique Chiu has begun a project that uses the border wall itself as a canvas. Since Trump's election, he has invited people from all over the world to come and paint messages that imagine an alternative vision of the border (Smith, 2018).

Towards border thinking

We are currently experiencing a particularly turbulent period in redefining the norms around borders. The performance of borders by Trump and Brexit supporters plays on fears that globalisation has caused states to lose control of their borders, coupled with racist discourses about both economic migrants and the threat of terrorism. While the virulent and violent nature of these border performances is new and striking, as we have argued, these trends in border policy are not in themselves new. Important antecedents to these developments have been the increasing militarisation of borders, the restrictions on the right to move and the expansion of border policing to the interior of nation-states. As such, what is significant is not so much the impacts of new border policies – though, of course, these are important – but the discursive intention of this more overt performance of the border.

Brexit has the potential to dramatically transform the configuration of borders between the UK and Europe, the UK and Ireland, and those on the island of Ireland. Moreover, it has the potential to alter the wider constellation of borders within the EU. Likewise, Trump's proposals to build the border wall with Mexico may exacerbate already-dangerous routes for migrants and give licence to racial tensions more broadly. Although these are potentially dangerous developments, it is important to see them within a continuum of a world increasingly characterised by starkly divided borders. This draws into view what Gilmartin calls 'border ontology' (see Naylor et al, 2018: 8–10). It is difficult to imagine a world without borders (Jones, 2016: 186). A 'border ontology' takes the existence of borders as a starting point, whether from a supportive or critical position. This view of the world reinforces a hierarchising of mobility, which inevitably places some people 'outside'. As Povinelli (2011) notes, late-liberal forms of governmentality normalise these distinctions between 'inside' and 'outside' and work to make them appear rational and humane. Normative discourses of borders thus hide the violence that borders create.

In this sense, the current moment also offers an opportunity to create an alternative imagination of borders. The explicit performance of bordering through Brexit and Trump has illuminated the inconsistencies and structural violence of current arrangements. The impact of these events on destabilising the consensus around borders constitutes what Walter Mignolo terms 'border thinking' – 'the moments in which the imaginary of the modern world system cracks' (Mignolo, 2000: 23; see also Naylor et al, 2018). The cracks created by Brexit and Trump have destabilised dominant ways of understanding borders and left new space in which alternative knowledge of borders can (re-)emerge and shape new political imaginaries.

Notes

1. Povinelli (2011: 25) defines 'late liberalism' as 'the shape that liberal governmentality has taken as ... a belated response to the challenge of social difference and the alternative social worlds and projects potentially sheltered there'.

2. Formed after French police cleared disparate camps located in the wooded area around the ferry ports and moved the refugees hoping to gain entry to the UK into one large camp. The 'Jungle' grew in size, numbers of inhabitants and levels of media coverage until it was violently demolished by French police in October 2016 (Davies and Isakjee, 2015; Mould, 2017).

THREE

Mobility

Introduction

This is the age of mobility (Papademetriou, 2007: 27). Contemporary mobility takes many forms (Adey, 2010); it includes the movement of people, things and ideas, and it also includes the infrastructure that makes movement possible. However, movement alone is not mobility. Tim Cresswell (2010: 19) says that mobility has three important and interconnected aspects. The first is physical movement: for example, a person moving from a rural area to an urban area, or between countries. The second is how that physical movement is embodied and experienced. The third is how that physical movement is represented; as an example, is it represented as a threat or as an opportunity? Adey (2010: 34–9) sums this up in a pithy statement: mobility is movement with meaning.

The advent of the 'new mobilities' turn in the social sciences and humanities has focused our attention on the centrality of mobility to contemporary life (Sheller and Urry, 2006). In this chapter, we are particularly concerned with the mobility of people, which we categorise in two ways. The first is travel:

moving from one place to another and, often, returning, where the stay away is for a short period of time. This broad definition incorporates a wide range of movement, including tourism and business travel. We are particularly interested in travel that crosses international borders. The second is migration. Like travel, this term is difficult to define, and includes internal and international migration, for temporary or permanent time periods, and with a range of different motivations. In this chapter, we are concerned with international migration, and we follow the United Nations' (UN's) definition of migration as movement for the purposes of settlement, for at least three months (United Nations Statistics Division, 2017). In this way, we distinguish between international travel and international migration on the basis of settlement intention and length of time. These definitions are, of course, partial and incomplete since the boundaries between a traveller and a migrant remain blurred. This is clearly shown by the diversity of mobile people listed by Sheller and Urry (2006: 207): 'asylum seekers, international students, terrorists, members of diasporas, holidaymakers, business people, sports stars, refugees, backpackers, commuters, the early retired, young mobile professionals, prostitutes, armed forces'. The current list of immigration schemes to the US and the UK also shows this diversity (see Table 3.1). For many, it is difficult to say where travel ends and migration begins.

Understanding the scale and extent of the physical movement of people brings many challenges. Two sets of statistics provide some insights. The first is data on tourism, provided by the World Tourism Organisation. In 2016, there were just over 37 million arrivals in the UK, 26% of whom were travelling for business. In the same year, there were just over 174 million arrivals in the US (World Tourism Organisation, 2017). The second set of statistics is data on migration. In 2016, the Office for National Statistics estimated that around 589,000 people immigrated to the UK (Office for National Statistics, 2017c). Around 1.18 million people immigrated to the US as legal

Table 3.1: Immigration schemes in the US and the UK

Scheme	US	UK
Employment-based schemes	E1: Priority workers E2: Professionals with advanced degrees/persons of exceptional ability E3: Skilled workers, professionals, unskilled workers E4: Certain special immigrants E5: Immigrant investors	Tier 1: Entrepreneur; Exceptional Talent; General; Graduate Entrepreneur; Investor Tier 2: General; Intra-Company Transfer; Minister of Religion; Sportsperson Tier 5: Temporary Workers Domestic Workers in a Private Household Visa
Family-based schemes	IR-1 to IR-5: Immediate Relative Immigrant Visa F1–F4: Family Preference Immigrant Visas	Family visa (partner, spouse, parent, child, private life)
Other schemes	Special Immigrant Visas Diversity Visas	UK Ancestry Visas

Sources: UK Government (2017) and US Department of State (2017).

permanent residents in 2016, but this does not include those who immigrated on a temporary basis (OECD, 2017). At the same time, of course, people were also moving from the US and the UK as tourists and emigrants. In 2016, there were almost 71 million visits abroad by UK residents and 80 million visits abroad by US residents (National Travel and Tourism Office, 2017; Office for National Statistics, 2018). At the end of 2015, it is estimated that around 5 million people born in the UK and 3 million people born in the US were living outside their country of birth (Migration Policy Institute, 2017). These numbers, though partial and incomplete, are important for showing the scale and complexity of the physical movement of people to and from the US and the UK.

While the numbers of people moving – as tourists, as business travellers and as migrants – are substantial, there are considerable differences in their embodied experiences. For elites – people with considerable economic, social and political capital – movement across international borders is frictionless. These 'internationally mobile wealthy individuals' (Koh and Wissink, 2018: 596) may have multiple homes, multiple citizenships and access to private jet services. Others may be privileged border crossers, with a passport that allows them visa-free travel. For example, citizens of 38 countries can, with some exceptions, spend up to 90 days in the US without a visa under the US Visa Waiver Program. Similarly, European Union (EU), European Economic Area (EEA) and Commonwealth nationals may enter the UK without a visa. In addition, the Registered Traveller Service in the UK or Trusted Traveler programmes in the US permit quicker border crossings, for a fee, for other privileged travellers. Special arrangements also exist between the US and the UK and some of their near neighbours. The Common Travel Area (CTA) permits passport-free travel between the UK and Ireland for UK and Irish citizens, and Canadian and American citizens do not need electronic travel authorisation (known as ESTA in the US, eTA in Canada) to travel between the two countries.

For many people on the move to the US and the UK, however, mobility is not frictionless. Instead, those without wealth or privileged citizenship face a number of obstacles to travel, which include long and/or cumbersome visa application processes, the high cost of visas, and the requirement to show access to significant levels of funds. Visa applications may be refused or, in some instances, people with the appropriate documents may be refused permission to enter the country. Encounters with border and immigration officials can often be upsetting. A survey of travellers in South Florida uncovered a range of troubling experiences, which included poor treatment, improper questioning, harassment, detention and deportation (Aranda and Vaquera, 2011). While these obstacles are often more stringent in relation to particular kinds of migrants and migration, they are also of significance for other mobile people, particularly those who are citizens of countries marked as problematic or troublesome. An Iranian man travelling to the US described how he adapted his behaviour in this context:

> I tried to sit silent and calm, without doing any extra moves. It was the same in the US Embassy. There are cameras all over the place. They would kick me out. I did not talk to anybody. I carefully followed their instructions. (Quoted in Khoshneviss, 2017: 317)

The representation of this physical movement of people also requires consideration. In particular, what we see is the creation and the articulation of hierarchies of mobile people, categorised on the basis of desirability. Thomas Faist has suggested that the key distinction is between migration and mobility. As he writes, 'labour migrants are understood as immigrants, whereas the highly skilled often are not' (Faist, 2013: 1642). So, in addition to internationally mobile wealthy people, highly skilled people are actively recruited by states around the world, and their movement is represented as mobility rather than as migration. Bridget Anderson (2013) writes that migration has become increasingly associated with poverty; in effect, the term 'migrant' is now understood to represent the global poor. If migrants are represented as those without sufficient capitals, then those with access to capitals are represented as cosmopolitan elites, as business travellers or as expatriates. Their mobility is facilitated, while that of migrants is restricted, both by states and state policies, and by border officials and border practices. The state is an important player in this process since exercising control over both mobility and its meaning offers a way for states to 'attempt to maintain their authority' (Glick Schiller and Salazar, 2013: 195). In effect, the representation of the physical movement of different types of people is integral to the process of hierarchisation, which occurs on the basis of social attributes such as nationality, class, race and gender, and varies across different spatial contexts. As a consequence of this process of hierarchisation, some people assume an unrestricted right to privileged mobility, while the global majority are keenly aware and frequently reminded of the different ways in which their mobility is constrained. Sheller (2016: 16) describes this as 'the disciplining of mobile subjects'.

In this chapter, we consider mobility – both travel and migration – in more depth. We begin by considering the US Travel Ban, first introduced in January 2017. We show how this attempt to restrict physical movement is based on long-standing representations of certain types of mobility as a threat, but also challenges assumptions around privileged access to mobility held by people in the US. We then discuss the role of migration in the Brexit campaign in the UK, as well as the consequences of the vote to leave the EU for UK nationals. We conclude with a brief discussion of the relationship between mobility and broader practices of inclusion and exclusion.

Travel and travel bans

On 27 January 2017, President Donald Trump signed an executive order, titled 'Protecting the nation from foreign terrorist entry into the United States' (The White House, 2017b). The order immediately suspended entry into the US for 90 days for people from Iraq, Iran, Syria, Yemen, Libya, Sudan and Somalia. There was resultant chaos at US airports and around the world as people were prevented from travelling to or entering the US. A series of legal challenges to the executive order temporarily halted its implementation, until a revised executive order, signed in March 2017, was partially affirmed by the US Supreme Court. In its June 2017 decision, the Supreme Court agreed that a 90-day ban on visitors from six countries – Iran, Syria, Yemen, Libya, Sudan and Somalia – could proceed temporarily. This ban was replaced, in September 2017, by a revised travel ban, which includes people from North Korea, Chad and Venezuela, excludes people from Sudan, and provides for extensive checks but not an outright ban on people from Iraq (Laughland, 2017). While the Supreme Court approved this ban in December 2017, it remains the subject of legal challenges in US courts (Laughland, 2017; McCarthy and Laughland, 2017).

The restriction of the right to travel for those who are perceived as threats or potential threats is a well-established practice. Travel bans take one of two general forms: the first is restrictions on the travel of particular individuals or groups; and the second is restrictions on all travel to and/or from a particular country (Hufbauer and Oegg, 2000). Restrictions are often imposed on the travel of (groups of) individuals. An example is the travel ban imposed on Gerry Adams, leader of Sinn Féin, who was prevented from travelling from Northern Ireland to Britain or the US during the 1980s and early 1990s. In contrast, blanket travel bans are less common and are 'primarily symbolic measures' (Hufbauer and Oegg, 2000: 15). The symbolism of the travel bans introduced by President Trump's executive orders has been explained with reference to his election campaign. In a statement issued in 2015, he called for 'a total and complete shutdown of Muslims entering the United States', claiming that 'there is great hatred towards Americans by large segments of the Muslim population' (quoted in Geier, 2015). In his election campaign, President Trump made explicit links between terrorism and immigration, particularly immigration to the US from Muslim-majority countries. The travel ban, which primarily targets citizens of Muslim-majority countries, is the manifestation of Trump's election promise to be tough on terror. He tweeted on 25 June 2016 that 'we must suspend immigration from regions linked with terrorism until a proven vetting method is in place', and reiterated this on 5 June 2017, saying that 'we need a TRAVEL BAN for certain DANGEROUS countries'.[1] President Trump also used terrorist attacks in other countries as grounds for advocating for his travel ban. In the aftermath of the September 2017 terrorist attack in London, he tweeted on 15 September that 'the travel ban into the United States should be far larger, tougher and more specific'. Trump had flirted with the idea of a regional travel ban in 2014, when he attempted to put pressure on President Obama to ban flights from countries affected by Ebola to the US. On occasion, his tweets connected Ebola and ISIS and, in both instances, his repeated argument was that stopping travel is a means of containing the related threat, whether that is the threat of infection or terrorism. Trump's tweets mirror many of the arguments that were made in the US from the 1870s onwards in the period prior to the passing of the Chinese Exclusion Act in May 1882. The lawyer H.N. Clement, one of those who portrayed Chinese immigration to the US as an 'invasion', argued at the time that 'A nation has a right to do everything that can secure it from threatening danger and to keep at a distance whatever is capable of causing its ruin' (quoted in Lee, 2002: 39). Clement's 'keeping at a distance' equates to Trump's travel ban, and both are manifestations of the broader practice of exclusion from the US, also applied at various times to other Asians, Southern and Eastern Europeans, and Mexicans (Lee, 2002: 51–2).

The latest travel bans thus follow a well-established practice in the US: regulating mobility in order to protect Americans and the idea of America (Lee, 2002: 56). A key difference, though, is the type of mobility that is being regulated. The Chinese Exclusion Act was directed at potential immigrants, while the contemporary travel ban, in addition to immigrants, also targets short-term visitors. This aspect of the ban initially caused considerable distress, and many early media reports focused on family members with visas who were prevented from entering the US. For example, a 69-year-old Iraqi man travelling to visit his son and grandchildren in California was detained for 12 hours and then sent back to Iraq. A Syrian woman travelling to Illinois to help care for her ill mother was sent back to Saudi Arabia, where she currently lived (Knickmeyer and Zoll, 2017). In addition to people with valid visas, some green card-holders were also refused entry. Due to a range of legal challenges to the first iteration of the travel ban, a number of changes were confirmed by Supreme Court decisions in June and July 2017. In particular, the June 2017 decision exempted people with 'bona fide' connections to the US from the travel ban. Judge Derrick Watson included a wide range of family relationships in his definition of 'bona fide' connections, including grandparents, grandchildren, brothers-in-law, sisters-in-law, aunts, uncles, nieces, nephews and cousins of people in the US. In July 2017, the Supreme Court affirmed his definition (Kennedy, 2017). This broad definition of 'family' certainly recognises the complexity of family structures and relationships. However, it also serves to further reinforce hierarchies of mobility, prioritising access for those with a pre-existing link to US legal residents or citizens. This is evident in statistics on the routes to legal permanent residency in the US. Of the just over 1 million people who received US green cards in 2016, around 68% did so because of family connections. In contrast, only 12% received green cards on the basis of their employment (Zong et al, 2018).[2]

Whether targeting Chinese or Muslim people, these are explicit bans on travel, framed as a response to concerns about security and well-being. However, in the contemporary US, there is another, less explicit, way in which mobility is restricted. Since 9/11, programmes such as Secure Communities and 287(g)[3] have shifted the responsibility for federal immigration enforcement from border patrols to state and local police. Allied with this, many states have become much more stringent in how they issue driving licences to immigrants, and have made it difficult or impossible for undocumented immigrants or some documented non-citizens to obtain a licence (López, 2004). Places where immigrants live have become sites of 'attempted migrant immobilization' because of how driving has become very risky for undocumented immigrants (Stuesse and Coleman, 2014: 54–6). The immobilisation happens in two ways: first, because of the difficulties in obtaining a licence; and, second, because of the threat of being stopped for a minor traffic incident that, in turn, could lead to deportation. Stuesse and Coleman (2014: 58) provide a very powerful description of this enforced immobility and its effect on people's everyday lives, which includes 'curtailing their use of automobiles, altering their driving patterns and schedules, and limiting activities of social reproduction, such as grocery shopping, educational activities, self-care pursuits, community and church participation, and socialization with friends and family to a bare minimum'. In effect, the displacement of federal immigration enforcement to the local level works as an implicit travel ban, limiting people's mobility in all but the most urgent situations, such as for the purposes of work. For migrants who are undocumented, being stopped while driving has consequences for mobility rights or restrictions. Those who are found to be in the US illegally are first incarcerated and then deported. Deportation levels from the US have risen considerably in the 21st century, with 4.2 million people deported – mostly to Latin America – from 2000 to 2013 (Price and Breese, 2016). With deportation comes another travel ban: people who are deported from the US are generally refused permission to re-enter the US for a 10-year period, in many instances separating them from family, friends and communities.

Despite the travel ban and the significant increase in deportations, migration and tourism to the US continue. Levels of immigration to the US continue to increase through the wide range of schemes detailed in Table 3.1. In 2016, 1.49 million people immigrated to the US, an increase of 7% from 2015 (Zong et al, 2018). In addition to immigration schemes, the US also has a range of other mobility schemes, such as student visas. The range of student visas includes F-1 visas for study at academic institutions and M-1 visas for study at vocational institutions. There were over 1 million international students registered in US higher education institutions during the 2015/16 academic year, 1.7% of whom were from countries affected by the original travel ban. They also feel trapped, being concerned that if they leave the US for professional or personal reasons, they may not be permitted to return (Rose-Redwood and Rose-Redwood, 2017). The travel ban appears to have affected the numbers of people travelling to the US as tourists. The Trump administration introduced a ban on electronic devices in the cabins of direct flights to the US from 10 countries, which, combined with the travel ban, resulted in a 20% drop in the number of travellers from the Middle East in the summer of 2017 (Maidenberg, 2017), as well as a more general decline in international arrivals in 2017 (US Travel Association, 2017). The resulting uncertainty has created difficulties for the US travel industry, which is a key contributor to the US economy, directly supporting 8.6 million jobs in 2016 (US Travel Association, 2016). As the US is finding out, enforced immobility also creates problems for the nation, in this instance, economic.

The migration problem

In the period before the UK referendum on membership of the EU on 23 June 2016, as well as during the referendum campaign, the issue of migration was central. Levels of immigration to the UK had been high for a number of years, both from within and from outside the EU. Intra-EU migration, specifically from the countries that had joined the EU in 2004, was particularly high. This is, in part, explained by the fact that the UK, Ireland and Sweden were the only three existing EU members that allowed immediate access to their national labour markets for citizens of the newer members. By 2017, almost 2 million people living in the UK were born in the 2004 Accession countries,[4] an increase of around 1.7 million since 2004 (Migration Observatory, 2017). While many moved to London and other large cities, A8 immigrants also moved to smaller towns and rural areas, working as agricultural labourers, in manufacturing and in services across the UK. This pattern of residential dispersal differed from previous waves of migration, and traces of A8 migration became visible in parts of the UK with limited or less obvious experiences of migration in the past. For many of those campaigning in favour of Brexit, stemming the flow of A8 migration, in particular, became a rallying cry. Leaving the EU would allow the UK to take back control of its borders, they argued. Membership of the EU meant that the UK had to adhere to the principle of free movement of people. Leaving would mean that the UK no longer had to automatically accept A8 migrants, and instead could be selective about who was admitted to the country, and under what conditions.

Campaigns in favour of Brexit, such as that run by the UK Independence Party (UKIP), emphasised the threat posed by migrants. These campaigns further stoked an anti-immigration sentiment that had been increasing over time, to the point that immigration was ranked as the most important issue in the country at the time of the referendum campaign (Goodwin and Milazzo, 2017: 451). Anti-immigrant sentiment was often directed against migrants from A8 countries and, at the time of the referendum, asylum seekers, refugees and so-called 'economic migrants', who were trying to get to the EU and the UK using a range of hazardous routes. Pro-Brexit campaigners emphasised the problem with EU-level agreements about the numbers of refugees to be relocated or resettled in the UK. In the process, though, they conveniently ignored the reality that the UK had already chosen not to participate in a range of EU mobility schemes, such as the Schengen Agreement. They also ignored the reality that the UK had sovereignty over migration from outside the EU, and that immigrant numbers from outside the EU – as permitted by UK government policies – were already substantial. In particular, the UK had been admitting significant numbers of international students to the country, and these international students were, in turn, providing much-needed revenue to UK educational institutions. The scale of immigration to the UK from A8 countries was represented as a problem caused by the EU. In contrast, since the 'problem' of international student migration had been caused by UK government policy, students themselves were represented as the cause of any difficulties. Pro-Brexit campaigners raised the issue of student visa overstayers to represent the way in which the UK had lost control of its borders.

The emphasis on A8 nationals, international students and 'refugees' as problematic migrants diverted attention from all the other migrants living in the UK. For example, there was significantly less attention given to migrants from the more established EU members, such as France or Italy. US nationals were not marked as migrants. Migration from other Commonwealth countries was rarely mentioned, particularly from majority white and English-speaking countries such as Canada and Australia. Also, Irish migrants, who have long represented one of the UK's largest migrant groups, were not included in discussions of the problems of intra-EU migration, despite the fact that migration from Ireland to the UK had increased considerably in the period prior to the referendum as a consequence of the severe recession in Ireland. The referendum campaign highlighted clear 'hierarchies of acceptability' (McDowell, 2009), articulated in terms of perceived cultural compatibility and skills such as English language proficiency and levels of education. The representation of acceptability differed, however, from the realities of how physical movement was permitted and facilitated. So, some intra-EU migrants were fine, while others were problematic. Similarly, some migrants from outside the EU were acceptable, while many were not. The constructed figure of the 'bad' migrant – someone who could not or would not integrate into UK society – was disassociated from the conditions under which that migrant arrived in the UK.

The precise identity of the 'bad' migrant has, of course, varied over time. Irish migrants were particularly problematic in the mid- to late 19th century, during the period following the Famines of the 1840s. Other 'problem' categories included

Jewish migrants and, later, migrants from the Commonwealth: Caribbean migrants (the so-called Windrush generation), expelled Ugandans, people moving from South Asia and, more recently, Muslims (Wills, 2017). The characteristics that marked migrants as 'bad' have rarely varied, though: disease, dirt, poverty, cultural incompatibility, violence and, latterly, terrorism. Thus, the current status of Irish migrants in the UK is worth considering in more detail since it illustrates this move from 'bad' to acceptable. While Ireland is a member of the EU, the current migration of Irish citizens to the UK is facilitated not just by EU membership, but also by the CTA. While the origins of and legal basis for the CTA remain uncertain, its implications are clear (Ryan, 2001): Irish citizens are free to travel to, live and work in the UK; they do not need special permission to do so; and they have access to the same rights as UK citizens in relation to voting and access to public services. This has resulted in ongoing and persistent migration from Ireland to the UK, which often peaks at times of economic crisis in Ireland. At different times, though, Irish migrants in the UK have experienced hostility, most recently, during the Troubles in Northern Ireland. The association of Irish migrants with Irish republicanism led to active discrimination, such as false conviction and imprisonment for terrorist activities. At the same time, Irish migrants were not identified as ethnically or culturally distinct. The first attempt to do so was through the inclusion of an 'Irish' category in the 2001 Census. At the time, this highlighted widespread experiences of poverty and ill-health, particularly among older Irish people. Recent Censuses suggest a polarisation of the Irish community in the UK, with poorer older people joined by recently arrived young professionals, many of whom work in highly paid employment in larger cities (Gilmartin, 2015: 51–2). In conjunction with the ceasefire in Northern Ireland, this may partially explain not just the exclusion of Irish migrants from the problem category, but also the growing involvement of people of Irish descent in anti-immigrant campaigns and political movements in the UK.[5]

The CTA is not just of relevance to Irish migrants in the UK; it also applies to migrants from the UK who live in Ireland. In the entire period since Irish independence, migrants with UK nationality have been the largest (until 2006) or second-largest (from 2011 on) migrant group in Ireland. If migrant status is measured in terms of place of birth, then migrants from the UK remain the largest group. The 2016 Census shows that over 270,000 people living in Ireland were born in the UK, compared to just over 115,000 born in Poland, the second-largest migrant group by birthplace (Central Statistics Office, 2017b). UK migrants in Ireland, like Irish migrants in the UK, avail of the provisions of the CTA, which gives them unrestricted rights to travel, live and work in Ireland. While Ireland is a key destination for outward migrants from the UK, it is just one of a number of popular destinations. In 2006, the Institute for Public Policy Research (IPPR) estimated that there were around 6 million Britons living overseas, close to one in 10. Ireland was the fifth most popular destination, following Australia, Spain, the US and Canada (Sriskandarajah and Drew, 2006: 17). In the EU, in addition to Ireland and Spain, there are significant populations of UK migrants living in France, Germany and Cyprus.

The extent of UK migrants living outside the UK was rarely problematised during the referendum campaign. Instead, discussions both during and after the referendum focused on the need to ensure that their rights were protected. The position of UK migrants in Spain received particular attention because of the specific issues associated with this migrant group. Many are older, having retired to Spain and purchased property that is now considerably lower in value – perhaps in negative equity – as a result of the property crash and recession. As EU migrants, they had also been entitled to use the Spanish health-care system, but their access to health care was coming under question as Brexit unfolded. The UK government insisted on the need to protect the rights of UK nationals living across the EU, such as those in Spain. Yet, the campaign to leave the EU was based on preventing a similar form of mobility: that of (certain) EU nationals to the UK. The mobilisation of anti-migrant settlement and the representation of migrants as threats are not unique to the UK or the US. Across the EU, for example, political parties with an explicit anti-migration stance are growing in popularity and expanding their support base. Such parties include the Freedom Party in Austria, the Danish People's Party in Denmark, the Finns Party in Finland, the National Front in France, Alternative für Deutschland (AfD) in Germany, Golden Dawn in Greece, Lega Nord in Italy and the Party for Freedom in the Netherlands, as well as UKIP and the Conservatives in the UK. Their growing popularity is shifting political discourse so that parties that were previously supportive of migration are now beginning to express doubts and concerns. This is clear in the public pronouncements of the Labour Party in the UK, who increasingly comment on the need for managed migration. In this way, anti-migrant sentiment is growing in reach, in the UK, the US and elsewhere. However, the specific constellation of attitudes to migration in the UK is worthy of attention, particularly the contradictions in representations of immigration and emigration. While immigration to the UK is hierarchised in accordance with mutable normative judgements, emigration from the UK is rarely made visible. When it is highlighted, it is from the assumption that emigration is unproblematic except for when it is restricted. As the IPPR commented, 'a Briton moving abroad is seen as part of the natural order of things' (Sriskandarajah and Drew, 2006: 91). This natural order means that there is limited attention to, or knowledge of, emigration from the UK. The same is true for emigration from the US, with 'data about the number of US citizens abroad ... meager and incomplete' (quoted in Croucher, 2009: 470). The common-sense understanding is that the UK and the US are immigrant-destination countries. Yet, millions of UK and US nationals live outside their country of origin/birth, and their right to do so is rarely questioned. An American woman who had been living in Mexico for 11 years told Sheila Croucher that 'They love us here', while other US migrants spoke about how their presence improved the economic and political situation in their new homes (Croucher, 2007: 27). This is despite the reality that Croucher outlined, where:

> [m]ost do not learn the local language and reside and socialize within an isolated cultural enclave.... Some live and work in the new country without proper documentation and have even been involved in the illegal transport of drugs across state borders. (Croucher, 2007: 23)

US or UK migrants are thus represented as expatriates or as lifestyle migrants, in contrast with the less salubrious representation of many immigrants to their countries. As one British migrant in Spain told the *Guardian* newspaper after the Brexit vote: 'expats are British, a foreigner is probably someone living, from another country, living in Britain. They become foreigners. The British are never foreigners wherever they go' (Kaye et al, 2017).

In addition to migration rights, UK and US nationals also assume that they will have relatively unimpeded rights to travel across international borders. This movement is facilitated by UK and US passports, which enable visa-free travel to over 170 countries (Kim, 2014). UK nationals regularly commute for work to, own holiday homes in and take short breaks in other EU countries. Brexit may make this more difficult, consigning UK nationals to the 'non-EU' lines at airports and ports. The likely inconvenience of future mobility restrictions became a common concern in public discussions about Brexit. In many cases, it was used as a justification for citizenship-shopping by UK nationals who were eager to preserve their EU mobility rights. Interestingly, many of those in search of alternative EU citizenship turned to Ireland, which offers citizenship by descent to those with a grandparent born on the island of Ireland or a parent who was an Irish citizen at the time of birth (Daly, 2001). One of these was Ivor Roberts, the former British Ambassador to Ireland. He was able to apply for Irish citizenship because he had one Irish grandmother. Sir Ivor told the *Irish Times* that he did this for convenience: 'We have a house in Italy', he said, adding that 'I don't want to find myself queuing to get through Rome airport every time I go there' (Murtagh, 2017).

The biopolitics of mobility

If, as Peter Adey asserts, mobility is movement with meaning, then we argue that the travel ban and the migration problem show how the meaning of mobility is currently being constructed. The recent US travel bans target specific groups of people on the basis of nationality and perceived religious affiliation. This is because of the association of these places and identities with the act of terrorism. The problem of migration in the UK works in a similar way by creating hierarchies of acceptability based on nationality and a range of embodied identities and skills. Both of these attempts to construct meaning have a longer trajectory: the treatment of Chinese migrants to the US and Irish migrants to the UK offer just two possible illustrations of how hierarchies are created and used to justify the exclusionary and/or discriminatory treatment of particular people and groups. What is evident now, in the US, the UK and elsewhere, is that certain types of mobility and, importantly, certain mobile people are increasingly being problematised for political purposes. Thus, the imposition of restrictions on people from so-called 'DANGEROUS countries' is a way of giving effect to political campaign promises around terrorism and migration. Similarly, 'taking back control' of migration and borders, the key promise of Brexit, is predicated on constructing some migrants as a threat, and political parties as having the potential to address that threat.

The representation of certain mobilities as threats has repercussions for the physical movement of people. For some, their privileged and elite status is unaffected. Indeed, in a globalised world where mobility remains a central and desired reality, their mobility rights may well be enhanced as a way of securing their position.[6] For those who plan to travel for a short period – like business travellers or tourists – mobility is often welcomed, in part, because of its association with potential economic gain, either through spending or innovation. As we show in Chapter Two, physical movement becomes more difficult for most people, with stringent visa and border controls, and with the expansion of border enforcement beyond the physical borders of states. In addition to Secure Communities and 287(g) schemes in the US, the EU is also engaged in a process of border externalisation, moving the management of its external border and migration to states such as Morocco, Mali and Mauritania (Casas-Cortes et al, 2015). Allied to this are regular changes to migration policy and practice, together with the contemporary expansion of temporary schemes for migration, making it increasingly difficult for many migrants to attain formal belonging in their new homes through the acquisition of citizenship. As a consequence, migrants who manage to cross borders face further difficulties in the form of protracted legal precarity, leaving them open to exploitation and formal expulsion through deportation. The resulting uncertainty, anxiety, stress and fear, combined with the threat of harm that is posed by growing levels of anti-immigrant sentiment and practice, mean that the embodied experiences of (some) mobile people, in places like the US and the UK, is increasingly negative.

The creation of hierarchies of mobile people, and their exploitation for political gain, leads us to insist on the importance of the biopolitics of mobility. A focus on the biopolitics of mobility emphasises the ways in which the right to mobility is associated with particular forms of life, while other forms of life have restricted, variable or no such rights. The overall purpose is to manage 'risky flows' – specific types of mobile bodies – while facilitating other flows that may be perceived as less risky (Topinka, 2016). In the current contemporary moment, the right to travel and migrate is increasingly being treated as a political favour to be bestowed on the select few. Paying attention to the processes by which hierarchies of mobile people and mobility rights are created, enforced and maintained – through physical barriers, through representations and through embodiment – is a pressing and urgent responsibility.

Notes

[1.] These and subsequent tweets attributed to President Trump are available at: http://www.trumptwitterarchive.com/

[2.] President Trump signalled his desire to restrict family migration in his State of the Union Address in January 2018, describing the 'current broken system' as 'chain migration', where 'a single immigrant can bring in virtually unlimited numbers of distant relatives' (The White House, 2018).

[3.] The 287(g) program was introduced in 1996. It allows the Department of Homeland Security to enter into formal agreements with state or local police departments who will then perform the function of immigration agents. The Secure Communities Program was launched in March 2008 and seeks to identify immigrants in US jails who could be deported under immigration law (see www.americanimmigrationcouncil.org for more details).

[4.] The 2004 Accession countries are the Czech Republic, Estonia, Hungary, Latvia, Lithuania, Poland, Slovakia and Slovenia (known as the A8 countries in the UK), together with Cyprus and Malta.

[5.] This includes Dublin-born Anne Marie Waters, who ran for the position of leader of UKIP in 2017.

[6.] Paradoxically, a new and growing body of research suggests that elite mobility may be illusory. Spence (2014) suggests that the super-wealthy may well confine themselves to a narrow geographical region when travelling by yacht, while Atkinson (2016: 1303) highlights the 'shielded mobilities' and 'delimited social encounters' of the super-rich in London.

FOUR

Belonging

Introduction

The meanings and practices of belonging to places have been affected by the era of globalisation. Brexit and the election of Donald Trump are not the first events to have an impact on belonging in this era, but they represent significant jolts, and the specific programmes of Brexit and the Trump administration indicate intentional reconfigurations of existing arrangements. In some cases, these political upheavals have served to intensify existing tendencies, or make existing practices more visible. In other cases, there are new problems, new connections made and new severances of existing connections.

Brexit and Trump have produced so much uncertainty that they are their own crises. They, and similarly disruptive moves for independence in Scotland or Catalonia, remind us that despite performances of state security at borders, the geopolitical order is always vulnerable to destabilisation. If we survey the history of modern Europe, for example, we can see that its borders and identities have changed frequently, with emergence of new nation-states, the disappearance of others, and other partitions and unifications generating new allegiances, championed by an expanding state. Tensions over existing borders and identities clearly remain, sometimes fed by resistance to narratives of unity. Nationalism has served as both an emancipatory and an authoritarian force (Bianchini, 2017). When it comes to questions of citizenship and belonging, both governments and individuals strategically navigate disputed cartographies.

The UK government and the Trump administration have made strong and explicit statements about bringing about change that will alter definitions of who belongs. What are the lasting impacts of such statements and the policies that may follow? What insights can we draw from the sentiments and structures that have been revealed by these crises? Mary Layoun (2001) has argued that ideas about citizenship are never more electrified than in a crisis. In these moments, the state makes an extraordinary effort to set out clear (and usually exclusionary) definitions to establish order, to instil fear and to promote political unity through purified ideas of who belongs. However, in the ordinary lives of citizens on the ground, belongings and allegiances may be much more complex and ambiguous. It is not the goal of this chapter, nor of this book, to predict what will happen in five, 10 or 40 years from now because of Brexit and Trump. Rather, we are interested in the insights that are exposed by these ruptures. As explored in Chapter Two, what inconsistencies or frailties do they reveal in the existing order?

Belonging and citizenship

Belonging is a reciprocally material and imaginative phenomenon, which is also geographical in all its forms. We feel a sense of belonging to places and to other people, often in terms of a defined collective. These connections to people and place are often themselves joined, as they are in the case of belonging to a nation-state, where we feel a connection to the place and to our fellow nationals. Even when we are considering the material, visceral experience of a place, place is always necessarily an idea as well (Tuan, 1977; Wood and Young, 2016). Encounter with the physicality of a place shapes the understandings, expectations and intentions of that place, and our ideas, in turn, shape the ways in which we understand and engage with the materiality of our worlds.

In this chapter, we focus on political forms of belonging, which are always and necessarily spatial, and specifically territorial. Ideas of belonging are attached to territories, and these territories may be official or unofficial, recognised or disputed. The different definitions of belonging and the varying scales at which belonging is imagined, understood and experienced may sometimes conflict with each other. For the purposes of examining practices of belonging to a nation-state, it must be remembered that the imagined nation and its cultural and social articulations are never as singular or united as they are commonly represented. Moreover, discourses of the nation and of its ideal citizens are used to discipline citizens' behaviour, and also to define, include and exclude members with varying degrees of belonging (Isin, 2001; White, 2006).

Expressions of national belonging are differently practised and articulated at local and regional scales. Access (or lack of access) to space, differential cultural capital and varying capacities to speak in everyday life at the local scale or even the scale of the individual body may enhance or constrain one's ability to identify willingly and/or be recognised by others as a member (Wood and Wortley, 2010). This membership or sense of belonging is often articulated as 'citizenship'. Although all citizens should be equal by definition, articulations of citizenship are gendered, sexualised, racialised and embodied in other particular ways that give some more rights to belong than others (Gilroy, 1991; Brown, 1995; Berlant, 1997; Yuval-Davis, 1997; Layoun, 2001; Longmore, 2003; Cohen, 2010; Simpson, 2014; Rankine, 2015; Gieseking, 2016). Some individuals and groups have the ability to represent the nation more than others. For example, middle-class white residents of Toronto unproblematically identify who they are and what they do as 'Canadian'; other people and other parts of Canada have, and are made to have, a stronger self-awareness of how they may not be representative of the whole.

National belongings operate within a larger context of other attachments beyond the nation. Maintaining connections to other parts of the world, while always possible, has been greatly facilitated by global infrastructure, from air travel to the Internet. For some, globalisation has transcended national belongings, supporting global yet individuated interactions and identities, and encouraging cosmopolitan, hybrid and multiple belongings (Isin, 2001; Ong, 2006). Globalisation and the Internet have also produced new spaces and new territorialisations, within which new forms of citizenship are produced, and new claims are made and negotiated (Isin and Ruppert, 2015). The neoliberal, global age thus increased the complexity of practices of citizenship and belonging, and unmoored them from some of their traditional territorialities. However, as noted for mobility in Chapter Three, this has occurred unevenly across space and across identities.

Belonging is not solely a personal or collective emotional attachment. The questions of who belongs and how this is determined are part of a political technology of identity construction. Belonging may be articulated in the language of formal categories as determined by the state, such as those of the Census (Anderson, 1983). Our understandings of the very nature of human identity and how it may be determined continue to shift. The application of DNA to establish identity is used not just in the connection with forensic criminal investigations, but also for establishing a link to 'peoples' and their 'original' geographies, as well as to legitimise family claims when crossing borders (particularly refugees). Facial recognition technology, fingerprints and retina scans are some of the methods used in the UK, US and elsewhere to certify that you are who you are when crossing borders, or simply to record the information for further tracking exercises (Sparke, 2006).

The articulation of belonging, in place and across time, happens on a shifting and dynamic political stage where individuals are affected by situations not of their making. The earlier considerations in this book of walls, borders and mobilities clearly link to questions of belonging and citizenship through their material and discursive processes of inclusion and exclusion. Our occupation of space in a territorial manner and our claims to legitimately be where we are — not the least of which is to claim a 'home' — are unavoidably political (Wise, 2000). Both governments and residents make claims about what can or should be 'home'. The right to belong is often understood as the right to inhabit, and vice versa, but in practice, these may be separated. In the contexts of Trump and Brexit, how are claims to a home affected? What political acts of belonging are possible?

Belonging and attachment to place are not only a state of being, but always a state of becoming, most visible in the adaptations of those who acquire a new sense of belonging in a new place. These ideas, attachments and identities are durable, but never fully stable or secure. They are always vulnerable to competing claims, at multiple scales. Individuals and groups also sometimes choose not to belong to a new environment, identifying themselves explicitly and exclusively with their previous place of residence, such as many British residents in Spain or the Americans residing in Mexico mentioned in Chapter Three.

People choose to belong or not to belong, because belonging is strategic. As Pierre Bourdieu (1984) articulated in his theory of taste, that which is seen as inherently good and valuable is determined by dynamics of social power. Our identities are the products of social practices that he terms 'structuring structures' (Bourdieu, 1984: 170). Beginning with the need to keep 'necessity at arm's length' (Bourdieu, 1984: 55), we accumulate various forms of 'capital' — economic, social, cultural — through relationships of alliance and distinction in order to achieve the highest degree of security and power that we can negotiate.

While Bourdieu's focus is on class-based social groups, his thinking equally applies to participation in national groups, where emotional and cultural attachments follow decisions of economic, social and political security and naturalise these choices as 'national identity' as if it were logical, even inevitable. This serves to hide the power dynamics and strategies that underlie citizenship choices; however, crises may bring these realities to the surface.

Brexit and belonging in the UK and Ireland

Less than a year after the referendum that set the decision to leave the European Union (EU) in motion, the prime minister of the UK, Theresa May, called a snap election. In that election of June 2017, her Conservative Party lost its majority and subsequently entered into a confidence-and-supply agreement with the leading unionist party in Northern Ireland, the Democratic Unionist Party (DUP), in order to maintain its control of Westminster. At that time, the DUP, which had campaigned for 'Leave' during the referendum, was also one of two main political parties (with Sinn Féin) stuck in a stalemate in the negotiation over a shared-power arrangement in the devolved government of Northern Ireland – still unresolved a year later.

The complex political situations to which Brexit immediately gave rise have much to teach us about belonging and citizenship in the early 21st century. Polities and identities that appeared to be settled and durable have been exposed as fragmented and fragile. National identities are always the products of history and politics, not merely cultural practices, beliefs or ideologies. Rather than seeing current political frameworks of belonging as culturally logical or the result of systematic and principled political engineering, it is more accurate to say that they are the result of stitching together the available pieces in a strategic fashion.

With the decision to leave the EU, what had been stitched into place within the UK has come undone. For the Conservatives, Brexit was an explicit rejection of the fluid identities arising from cosmopolitan outlooks or globalised attachments. At the first post-referendum Conservative Party Conference in October 2016, Theresa May declared: 'If you believe you are a citizen of the world, you are a citizen of nowhere'. Realities on the ground, however, are more complex, and thus Brexit sent belonging and citizenship into a tailspin.

The EU enables citizens of its member states to live and work throughout the region. The UK has millions of long-term EU residents without UK citizenship whose permission to remain will be disputed, and who at the very least are in need of a system to resolve their status. Similarly, about 900,000 UK citizens consider themselves permanent residents of other EU countries (Office of National Statistics, 2017a); they may lose their residence rights when the UK exits the EU. Many of them have strong attachments to their place of residence regardless of their formal citizenship. The country where they hold citizenship may feel relatively foreign, and relocation for them and their families may constitute a significant cultural change.

The tangled arrangements of the UK and Ireland is another example of a historically specific, strategic stitching–together of geography and identity, and Brexit creates further difficulties for their relationship, as the fallout of the June 2017 snap election made more visible. It complicates the terms of identity and citizenship rights negotiated in the 1998 Good Friday Agreement (GFA) for residents of Northern Ireland, and it affects the decision-making context for residents of Britain who have Irish ancestry. Both of these may, in turn, have serious consequences for Ireland in the near future. Given the complexity and potential impact, the EU identified the UK's relationship with Ireland as one of three key areas to prioritise in Brexit negotiations.

The Common Travel Area (CTA) between Britain and Ireland, raised in earlier chapters, was established in the wake of the declaration of the Irish Free State in 1922; the UK's response was to recognise the island as a Dominion within the British Commonwealth. The UK's assertion of the Irish Free State as a Dominion made Irish citizens, in the eyes of British law, British subjects. When Ireland declared itself a Republic in 1948, the UK decreed the following year that Ireland would not be treated as a 'foreign country', and maintained for Irish citizens the same rights as the citizens of Commonwealth countries, which included the right to immigrate. When controls were brought in for the rest of the Commonwealth in 1972, an exception was again made for Ireland (O'Carroll, 2016). In law, the two countries do not see each other's citizens as 'foreign nationals'. They maintain immigration, employment and some voting rights in the other country.

However, because the CTA was subsumed into a larger geography of free movement – when the UK and Ireland entered the Common Market together – if the UK leaves both the customs union and the internal market as planned, Brexit will establish a new hard border at the edge of the EU, and the status of people born in Ireland but residing in a post-Brexit UK (389,000 as of 2016) is uncertain (Office of National Statistics, 2017b). It is also unclear as to how the CTA could remain in force for UK citizens residing in Ireland, who remain one of the largest migrant groups there.

The political history of Northern Ireland produced a particular constellation of citizenship rights and practices, set in complex domestic realities and regional relationships with Ireland and the UK. The conflict in Northern Ireland arose between two communities divided not only by religious and ethnic identity, but, more importantly, by mutually exclusive nationalist aspirations (McGarry and O'Leary, 2006a, 2006b). The peace established via the GFA was more than an 'inclusive civic nationalism'; it is a consociational agreement that built on and extended the Irish–British binationalism already present in order to create a 'bespoke' consociationalism (McGarry and O'Leary, 2006b) that was equally of both the UK and Ireland, and of neither of them.

The GFA is, in fact, two agreements: one among political parties of Northern Ireland with the endorsement of the British and Irish Governments; and one between the UK and Ireland. It was arrived at with the active assistance of not only the UK and Irish governments, but also political representatives from the US, Canada and the EU; the involvement of these external actors was understood to be critical to its success (McGarry and O'Leary, 2006b). The GFA was put to a referendum vote in both Northern Ireland and the Republic of Ireland in May 1998. It received support from both referenda and all major political groups in both countries, with the significant exception of Prime Minister May's new government partner, the DUP, who refused to endorse it.

The GFA integrated the Republic of Ireland into the governance of Northern Ireland in several ways, and established all-Island governance practices, including the development of a joint parliamentary forum of the Northern Ireland Assembly and the Oireachtas (the Irish Parliament), several all-island governance bodies, and the British–Irish Inter-Governmental Conference (McGarry and O'Leary, 2006a). These corollaries of the GFA created transnational political geographies, which changed the meaning and practice of sovereignty in these countries to something more fluid. This fluidity synchronised not only with the competing and overlapping belongings that exist in Northern Ireland, but also with belongings within the larger region of the EU. Institutionalising these overlaps in the GFA was possible because of the characteristics of shared sovereignty of the EU, and these institutions and relationships were, in turn, facilitated by shared membership in the EU and in the European Court of Human Rights.

With regard to addressing issues of belonging, the GFA recognised both the majority wish of Northern Ireland residents to remain in the UK and the majority wish of the island of Ireland to be united. With the open-ended recognition of the possibility of a decision to unite Northern Ireland with the Republic of Ireland, the GFA stated that Northern Ireland residents with one parent who was either a British or Irish citizen, or otherwise a permanent resident, had the right to 'identify themselves and be accepted as Irish or British or both' as a 'birthright' (*GFA*, 2.1.vi) and affirmed that they could thus hold either or both formal citizenships. As over 95% of Northern Ireland residents were born in Northern Ireland (89%) or in the Republic of Ireland or Britain (6.7%), this covers almost the entire Northern Ireland population (UK 2011 Census). As of the 2011 (UK) Census, 59% of Northern Ireland residents hold a UK passport, 21% hold a Republic of Ireland passport and 1.7% hold both (19% do not hold either). The small number holding both passports suggests a bifurcated nature of geopolitical allegiances in Northern Ireland, but those choices were made in a context where there was little to no difference between them in terms of the mobility that they enable. Without knowing the current totals, we nonetheless know that those numbers have changed: the number of applications from Northern Ireland for an Irish passport was 53,718 in 2015, 67,972 in 2016, and 81,752 in 2017 (an increase of 51% in two years) (Department of Foreign Affairs and Trade, 2018).

Ireland also has a Foreign Births Register, which provides access to Irish citizenship for people born outside Ireland who have a grandparent or great-grandparent who was born in Ireland, or a parent who was an Irish citizen at the time of birth. If the ancestor is registered, a descendant is automatically an Irish citizen on the date of registration, and may apply for a passport. As Mary Daly points out, this provision was intended to encourage the descendants of Irish emigrants to return to Ireland but was initially rarely used. Only 16,500 people were granted Irish citizenship by descent in the 50 years from 1936 to 1986 (Daly, 2001: 403). By contrast, in 2015, there were 46,242 applications from Great Britain alone, and a further 64,996 in 2016 and 81,287 in 2017. (It is worth noting that Northern Ireland, with its population of just 1.8 million, saw more passport applications in each of the last three years than Great Britain [population 60 million].) It is estimated that there are 6 million UK citizens who are eligible to apply for an Irish passport – a number that exceeds the current population of Ireland.

The situation is further complicated by the fundamental changes to Irish citizenship that have taken place in the past 20 years. The introduction of birthright citizenship into the Irish Constitution in 1999, following the acceptance of the GFA, lasted only five years. The 2004 citizenship referendum, which followed a moral panic about 'citizenship tourism', again altered the basis of Irish citizenship. Since 2004, children born in Ireland no longer have birthright citizenship unless at least one of their parents is an Irish national (White and Gilmartin, 2008).

Built on the historically constituted political geographies of the Irish nation, Irish citizenship reflects the complexity of citizenship in practice. While it is far from immune from romantic patriotism, Irish citizenship has strong elements of strategic pragmatism, or 'responsible realism', as McGarry and O'Leary (2006b: 254) have characterised consociation in Northern Ireland. Furthermore, while the consociational arrangement in Northern Ireland is not cosmopolitanism, it nevertheless allows for multiplicity in the institution and practice of citizenship, and disturbs the usual simple territorial borderings. It is not only the material form of the border that has been made invisible, as noted in Chapter Two; the imagined border that divided political belongings was also made to disappear.

The new interest in Irish citizenship in the wake of Brexit raises some questions about the future character of Irish nationalism, particularly when we add in the possibility of reunification. Those claiming citizenship via Irish ancestors are likely to be white and Catholic. Will this be reasserted as a more 'authentic' Irishness? In news media and on social media, there are already debates about whether ancestral applicants have enough of a connection to be 'proper' citizens, with some signs of resentment. Discussions about 'purity' of identity are worrisome, and create an environment where it is much more difficult for those with other ethnic backgrounds who are resident in Ireland to express their belonging in practice, and to claim an equal social and political voice.

Northern Ireland raises a complicated question for a post-Brexit UK's citizenship practices. In December 2017, the EU and the UK reached a preliminary agreement on citizens' rights, the Irish border and the financial settlement. The parties have agreed that EU and UK citizens resident in each territory at the date of withdrawal will be entitled to remain and apply for permanent residence if they do not already hold it. The agreement also reasserted a shared commitment to uphold the GFA, including its provisions for Irish and British citizenship claims as a birthright (European Commission, 2017). The details as to how these citizenship rights will be arranged, and how migration during the transition period will be handled, are to be determined in the next phase of negotiations. If the UK does not provide equal rights for EU citizens as for UK citizens, then residents of Northern Ireland who have chosen Irish citizenship based on their residence within that part of the UK according to the GFA will not have equal citizenship in their own country of birth and residence. Will Irish citizens continue to receive special recognition throughout the UK? Will the added instability of Brexit continue to contribute to the instability of the power-sharing agreement in the Northern Ireland Assembly? Is consociationalism now incompatible with a UK that is not a member of the EU? Both Tony Blair and former Taoiseach Bertie Ahern have emphasised the role of the EU in enabling the extraordinary 'diplomatic game of Jenga' that is the GFA. As Blair said in his 1998 address on the GFA to the Oireachtas, this is 'all about belonging', and it worked because it 'was underpinned by European integration' (Morrow and Byrne, 2016: 31).

The emotional attachments and entanglements expressed by ordinary citizens in the various parts of the UK are bound to a strong spine of pragmatics: the desire to maintain access to the EU. Although claiming these Irish passports or returning to Ireland is dismissed by some as 'opportunistic', so-called opportunism is a fundamental character of formal citizenship. Despite its many patriotic window dressings, we need to see citizenship choices as political positions and as strategic, and not moralise or romanticise them.

Moreover, as we contemplate old and new belonging to Ireland, we must remember that Ireland and Irish identity are not singular or static entities. For example, the success of the 2015 same-sex marriage referendum, in the context of increased urbanisation and secularism, reflects a modernisation that is shifting what it means, in practice, to be Irish in Ireland. The globalisation of its trade since the 1990s, and the shift in migration, particularly newcomers to Dublin, have also introduced a new diversity and sense of cosmopolitanism, even as the 2004 referendum restricted the ability of non-ethnically Irish people to claim citizenship for their Irish-born children (Gilmartin, 2008; White and Gilmartin, 2008). Legally and socially, 'Irishness', like any national identity, remains in flux.

These ideas and practices of belonging also occur within the context of the fragmenting of the EU project in recent years, where the response to the global financial crisis has created new divisions between core and peripheral member states. This has given rise to both a Left critique of the EU as a neoliberal institution and to a Right populism seeking to define who does and does not belong within national and EU borders. Both were at work in the Brexit referendum campaign. As such, local and regional deliberations about citizenship in the UK and Ireland are entangled with and affected by debates about belonging and the contested reconfiguration of the EU.

The fragility of belonging in the US

Questions of formal citizenship, while not irrelevant, give us only a little insight into the situation in the US. Naturalisation rates within the US began to rise significantly in the 1980s and 1990s. In large part, this was due to legislation that granted permanent resident status to some 'illegal aliens' and other laws that made accessing public services more difficult for non-citizens (Witsman and Baugh, 2016; Zong and Batalova, 2016). Given the high estimates of irregular residents, applications for citizenship have a stronger correlation to policy than to a sense of belonging, although these are not entirely separable. Zong and Batalova (2016) have argued that a sharp increase in early 2016 was caused, in part, by 'a citizenship awareness campaign launched by the White House Task Force on New Americans, as well as a desire to vote in the 2016 national elections'. As seen with Brexit, the desire to participate and the desire to secure one's residential status are both strategic and emotional. There are some early indications that Trump's immigration policies (or attempts to introduce them) are increasing naturalisation applications as lawful permanent residents seek a more secure position (Jordan, 2017).

The 1990s were also the beginning of a steep rise in the number of unauthorised immigrants in the US, peaking in 2007 at over 12 million people, which was almost four times the estimate in 1990 (Krogstad et al, 2017). Mexican nationals constitute about 50% of the figure, although their proportion of the total is shrinking. The vast majority (8 million of the 2015 estimate of 11 million) are in the workforce, constituting 5% of the total US civilian workforce (15% of construction workers and 26% of farm workers). Approximately two thirds of these unauthorised immigrants have been in the country for more than 10 years.

On the other hand, in 2016, over 5,400 Americans living outside the US renounced their citizenship. Since 2010, when fewer than 2,000 gave up their citizenship, and when the US Congress introduced tougher rules and penalties about foreign income on tax returns (which all American citizens, regardless of residence, are required to file), the numbers renouncing citizenship have grown rapidly. Since Trump's election, there have been anecdotal reports that the number of inquiries for assistance with renunciation had increased further still. The ties of belonging within the US, however, are coming undone even more quickly and seriously.

The US, a highly fragmented and fractured polity, has traditionally been held together through strong central and centralist institutions and patriotic discourse that draws explicitly on the inclusive, universalist language of the constitution. The calls for patriotism from President Trump are rooted not in that constitutionalism, but rather in abstractions of some of its concepts, re-contextualised in a vague but protectionist way. Despite the invocation of MAGA (Make America Great Again), his language is divisive, discriminating among different Americans, along a variety of identity axes, in a way not seen in US political campaigns since at least the Second World War (although there have been other campaigns with racist elements). Usually, the distinctions and insults run along partisan lines as differences between 'liberals' and 'conservatives'. In the 2016 campaign, Trump presented the other side as outsiders, whether he was speaking of his opponent, the Democratic candidate Hillary Clinton, or the many groups of people he described as undeserving of residence or citizenship in the US.

What has Trump's election revealed about ideas and practices of citizenship in the US? Some would say that it has rejuvenated it: his election and policy initiatives have been met with large-scale public protest, an avalanche of phone calls and emails to political representatives, and strong attendance at town-hall meetings with those representatives. Many citizens have explicitly rejected his discriminatory rhetoric and reasserted an inclusive narrative of America as a land of equality and opportunity for all.

However, the triumph of Trump reveals the endurance and regrowth of other narratives of America that have their roots in a variety of intolerant soils, most notably, white supremacy and some strains of socially conservative Christianity. These are narratives unmistakably marked by intolerance: racism, sexism, ableism, homophobia and transphobia have all been articulated in no uncertain terms. At the start of his campaign in June 2015, Trump accused Mexico of sending 'drugs, crime and rapists' to the US. In November 2015, Trump physically mocked a disabled reporter, Serge Kovaleski of the *New York Times*, during a speech at a campaign rally. In an interview on Fox News in January 2016, he said that he would consider appointing justices to the Supreme Court who would overturn same-sex marriage. He publicly judged several women as unattractive, including his opponent, and campaign merchandise with misogynistic images and slogans were regularly worn and sold at his rallies.

As noted in Chapter Two, some of Trump's worst rhetoric came as he drew a discursive hard border around the US in the name of security, and in the interests of shoring up the privileges of supposedly beleaguered ethnic national populations. The comments about 'drugs, crime and rapists' from Mexico were partnered with his calls to build a wall at the Mexico–US border. In August 2016, in a campaign speech in Phoenix, Arizona, he used borders and the language of citizenship to demonise immigrants: 'our immigration system is worse than anybody ever realized', he said:

> Immigration reform ... should mean improvements to our laws and policies to make life better for American citizens.... It's our right, as a sovereign nation, to choose

immigrants that we think are the likeliest to thrive and flourish and love us. (Transcript from the *New York Times*, 2016)

He directly attributed violent crime to what he alleged was the weak screening of immigrants:

> Countless innocent American lives have been stolen because our politicians have failed in their duty to secure our borders.... I have met with many of the great parents who lost their children to sanctuary cities and open borders.... Countless Americans who have died in recent years would be alive today if not for the open border policies.... The perpetrators were illegal immigrants with criminal records a mile long, who did not meet Obama administration standards for removal. (Transcript from the *New York Times*, 2016)

Much of Trump's exclusionary language was specifically Islamophobic, expressing the desire for, as noted in Chapter Three, 'a total and complete shutdown of Muslims entering the United States'.

Immediately following his inauguration, it was clear that Trump and his administration would continue the campaign strategy of using divisive and exclusionary identity politics. Appointments to his cabinet included individuals who had been outspoken against civil rights and equality, often rooted in religious beliefs. He made the implementation of a 'Muslim ban' at the border a priority. In July 2017, Trump gave a speech to New York law enforcement in which he intensified his negative descriptions of immigrants, describing the removal of unauthorised immigrants as the 'liberation' of towns and cities ('bloodstained killing fields') from gang violence. That same month, Trump announced that he was banning transgender soldiers from all service in the US military (they had only been serving openly since 2016). The symbolism of military service intensifies the discursive impact of this exclusion as it marks transgender bodies as both unfit to serve and incapable of representing the nation. While disabled people have been subject to less overtly discriminatory rhetoric, Trump and the Republican Congress have sought to reduce or eliminate education, health care and social welfare programmes on which disabled people depend (Bagenstos, 2017), and in February 2018, the House voted to water down the Americans with Disabilities Act by increasing the difficulty of holding businesses accountable to provide accessible services (DeBonis, 2018).

There could hardly be a sharper contrast than with the participation of Canada's Prime Minister Justin Trudeau and Irish Taoiseach Leo Varadkar, himself openly gay, walking in the Montreal Pride Parade together, as mentioned in Chapter Two. Widely received as a progressive gesture, their public participation in Pride contributed to a narrative of diverse and inclusive citizenship. Trump's narrative has more in common with dominant narratives in the UK. As noted in Chapter Two, constructions of 'unwanted Others' were part of both Trump's election campaign and the pro-Leave Brexit campaign. As discussed in Chapter Three with reference to the changing representations of Irish people, transitioning from 'bad' to 'good' migrants, ideas of who is or is not 'like us' are durable yet still malleable, and used strategically.

Trump's discourse has revealed and widened existing fractures as the president's language and the silence from his fellow party members encourage a greater tolerance for intolerance. This legitimation of everyday racism has taken more extreme forms, such as the public displays of organised white nationalism, including torch-lit marches in Virginia. The growing prominence of racist, sexist, ableist and anti-queer language and policy serves to restrict access to the public sphere for the excluded 'Others'. As Bagenstos (2017: 418) has argued with specific reference to disabled people:

public debate about social welfare programs often revolves around questions of citizenship – in particular, whether receipt of benefits serves as a recognition of one's status as a full citizen, or instead whether it stands as an obstacle to citizenship status.

In many instances, policy and the space and language of its public debate limit the ability of individuals and communities to participate and, more broadly and insidiously, erode their capacity to feel that they belong and to identify themselves as Americans.

It must also be noted that the apparent acceptance of exclusionary narratives of citizenship in the mainstream has endangered many citizens. Hate crimes and the number of organised hate groups in the US rose in 2015 and 2016 in tandem with the presidential campaign, particularly Islamophobic organisations and crimes. The Southern Poverty Law Center identified almost 900 incidents of hate or bias in the 10 days following the election. A study of 13 cities noted a further 20% jump in the first part of 2017 (Center for the Study of Hate and Extremism, 2017). Hate crimes are also up in the UK since the Brexit campaign, where there was a spike in incidents against many groups, especially Eastern Europeans, in the immediate wake of the referendum. The Home Office recorded a rise of 30% in reported incidents between March 2016 and March 2017 (BBC News, 2017); some of these crimes are understood to be responses to terrorist attacks in London and Manchester. Layoun's theory of the assertion of narrow, defensive definitions of the citizen in times of crisis appears to be well founded.

Trump's rhetoric targets those wanting to migrate to the US as well, but his categorisations primarily serve to exclude or disrupt the belonging of millions of Americans. He draws a map of walled borders, and asserts a singular 'true' America lost in the past, in need of reclamation. We should nevertheless remember that Trump's geography is not the only map: there remains a strong sense of belonging by Mexicans and Mexican-Americans to the area of the south-west US that was historically Mexican territory, to say nothing of the many indigenous claims and attachments to place.

Practices and feelings of belonging in the US, always frayed, have begun to unravel, with the active encouragement of Trump. The explicit disrespect for and demonisation of individuals and groups, justified merely by their identities, renders them second-class citizens or inadmissible. Already-complex histories of belonging to the territory of the US and to its collective as a 'nation' have become more difficult to come to terms with.

Citizenship and belonging in the 21st century

That formal citizenship is a strategic and pragmatic attachment is not unique to the 21st century. It has always been strategic, and its use by elites is a given, with a remarkable privileged flexibility there that is unavailable to others. Similarly, its use by the middle-class political and economic establishment as a tool of governance and as a gateway or barrier to global mobility reveals the strategic leveraging of formal status in multiple directions and at multiple scales. Patriotism is stitched on after the fact: in part, invented through the construction of civic identities and mythic histories; and, in part, tacked onto to the everyday practices of belonging and attachment to place of ordinary people. While material, grounded practices are formative of identity (Stahaeli et al, 2012; Wood and Young, 2016), they exist in a charged political field that must be strategically negotiated.

When we speak of citizenship, it is often to invoke that formal status of membership in a nation-state and its attendant rights and privileges, such as residence rights and suffrage. However, citizenship is more fully understood as the relationship between the governor and the governed. It is a technology of governance, a practice as much as a status. This includes the formal status of citizenship, but does not limit itself to it. The recognition of a constantly negotiated relationship explains how those with formal citizenship can nevertheless have their rights disregarded, as well as how those without formal citizenship or even legal status may nevertheless successfully make claims against a governor. This framework also broadens the idea of government beyond the state to include other actors with the capacity to insist on behavioural compliance, as well as to include the complexity of governmentality and self-governance. Citizenship also goes beyond practices of law as the concept and its emotional attributes are mobilised by governors to encourage, discipline or even compel behaviours that have nothing to do with obeying the law (White, 2006), such as vaccination and other public health practices, environmental stewardship, and so on.

As the work of Michael Peter Smith (2001) has documented, citizenship rights have never been strictly bound by status or territory: non-citizens successfully claim rights in places where they have no legal status; and citizens successfully claim rights from outside the territory. Consociationalism, as in Northern Ireland, demonstrates that citizenship status and national belonging may be structured territorially in plural and overlapping ways. Formal citizenship and dominant geopolitical orders are only part of the picture.

It is important to keep visible the ways in which citizenship and its attendant obligations, identities and ideas of belonging are leveraged by governments, as well as the ways in which citizens are similarly able to leverage their own power to pressure and persuade, ensuring that the sovereignty claimed by their governments is contingent in practice on the consent of the governed. A governor, including the state, is that which it asserts itself to be, but also what the governed successfully demand that the governor be. Thus, this discussion of citizenship in the wake of Brexit, Trump and other exclusionary events must be seen as having two sides – the governors and the governed – both of whom have differential capacity to affect each other, which varies according to circumstance in often unpredictable ways.

The important point is that neither side has a monopoly on the definition of citizenship.

The act of claiming citizenship is itself an effort to govern from the bottom up, to reset the terms of political belonging within a nation-state or across borders. These decisions, particularly in a moment of crisis, are strategic negotiations towards distinguishing and privileging oneself within perceived possibilities. Individual citizenship choices are frequently rooted in pragmatic reasoning related to future security, mobility, family ties and civil rights like voting. The national imaginary that captures those citizens, however, is commonly built on narratives of values, principles and character, resting on historical myths that classify insiders and outsiders.

Faced with restrictions on their EU mobility and uncertainty regarding their status within the UK, those with claims to Irish citizenship through residence in Northern Ireland or through their ancestry are strategically choosing security. While some are comfortable with the pragmatics of the choice, many others seek to justify their decision to apply through highlighting the significance of childhood memories, a desire to reconnect with their family roots or a generalised 'pride' in their connection to Ireland. Still others are challenging the applicants, arguing that they do not have a 'real' connection to Ireland.

There is always going to be some level of anxiety around the determination of who 'belongs' and who has the right to determine that. It is an eternally contested situation because we purport to create polities that we allege to be 'unified'. Ideas of united polities are myths perpetrated strategically by elites for their own political and social sovereignty (Isin, 2001). Employing the ideas of unity and loyalty is a disciplinary tactic, particularly as a condition of inclusion or belonging.

Citizenship in a neoliberal globalised world is about more than open borders and cosmopolitan belongings. The fluidity and multiplicity of identities and practices emerged in the context of reduced obligations from the state and an increased insistence on self-sufficiency and personal responsibility. Those with access to greater mobility through citizenship, whether through financial means, residence or ancestry, benefit. Movement among EU nation-states, for example, stands in sharp contrast to the restrictions imposed on those outside 'Fortress Europe'; as mobility among wealthier nations increased, the walls between them and the rest of the world became thicker and higher.

Domestically, these shifting practices of citizenship have served to disadvantage those whose circumstances leave them more dependent on the state. The erosion of the welfare state, particularly in the areas of the privatisation of health care and housing, has increased the material precarity of many individuals and communities. Their capacity to participate and thrive is diminished, and their sense of belonging, their sense of being a member of a national community that expresses *care* for them, is similarly diminished (see Cohen, 2010). While neoliberal, globalised citizenship has expanded horizons for some, it has reduced them for many others. Discourses of citizenship are part of constituting these class divisions, and these discourses are, moreover, used to seek legitimation for the uneven socio-economic outcomes for different groups.

What the crises of Brexit and Trump reveal, among other things, is liberal democracies' continued inability (and perhaps lack of intention) to include the diversity of all members of its polities and to prepare for the uneven impact that such crises will bring. However, importantly, Brexit and Trump are not the cause of this political weakness, although they weaken it further. The current crises are actively feeding anxiety and precarity, disrupting and narrowing the space in which people make their individual strategic decisions. This anxiety and precarity, the fragility of belonging, and the need to be strategic about allegiances, however, are built into the system. States have attempted to constitute ideal citizens through strategic inclusion and exclusion; ideas of national identity have been employed to constitute states. The UK and the US have been the world's most powerful liberal democracies, but their inherent precarity and inequity has been brought to the surface once again. Territorially defined Western nation-states as we know them may be breathing their last, while simultaneously resurging with an isolationist vengeance.

FIVE

Conclusion

In the current political moment, a combination of liberal democracy and neoliberal capitalism has become the dominant state model for much of the world. The democracy/neoliberal consensus emerged from the fall of the Berlin Wall and the decline of state socialism in the latter half of the 20th century. These changes enabled the thickening of geopolitical relationships and globalisation processes, which were supported by new legal and technical arrangements, such as the North American Free Trade Agreement (NAFTA) between the US, Canada and Mexico, or the expansion of the European Union's (EU's) sphere and scale of influence. Until the advent of the global financial crisis, this consensus appeared to hold. As the crisis developed, though, the problems with neoliberal capitalism became increasingly obvious: people lost homes when mortgages were foreclosed; they lost work when unemployment levels soared; and they lost income when wage rates were cut. States were reluctant to recognise the role of neoliberal policies in this crisis, even though Peck (2012: 630) insists that periodic returns to crisis are caused by the failure of 'successive waves of neoliberal reform to generate sustainable economic, social or environmental development'. Instead, most states responded by introducing austerity measures, which included a contraction of public sector spending. This had a disproportionate effect on those people who were already struggling to get by.

For many commentators, states had played a central role in the intensity of the global financial crisis because of their lack of regulation of markets and capital in their support of neoliberal capitalism. Yet, rather than directly address this issue, politicians and political parties sought other explanations for the economic difficulties that their citizens were experiencing. In particular, the attention shifted to the role of migrants in many Western liberal democracies. In states such as the UK and the US, among others, politicians and pundits increasingly began to link economic woes to the presence of migrants, despite little in the way of evidence supporting this link. Migration and migrants became a target for those who sought to divert attention from broader economic, political and social dysfunction, and for those who sought to understand the difficulties that they were experiencing in their everyday lives.

In this book, we have shown that migration and citizenship rights are again coming under sustained attack. States have long used their control over migration and citizenship to demonstrate their power, while, at the same time, espousing liberal-democratic values that run contrary to these acts of control. Historically, for example, the UK positioned itself as a champion of democracy and enlightenment during its violent imperialist period, while displaying active antipathy towards immigration and diversity. The US self-identified as a haven for 'masses yearning to be free', while, at the same time, imposing immigration bans, quotas and exclusion. In the current era, we again see the construction of the 'dangerous' migrant who poses a threat to the state, though the threat has taken on a new form. Isabell Lorey identifies the migrant threat, post-9/11, as being framed in two, interlinked ways. The first is the threat of terrorism, while the second is the threat posed to the economic security of privileged states (Lorey, 2015). While both threats are highlighted in the US and the UK, they receive different levels of attention in the two states. Terrorism is the focus of many of President Trump's public statements and tweets in relation to migration, while economic security is more likely to be mentioned by politicians and pundits in the UK. In both the US and the UK cases, current or aspirant political leaders employ their responses to the issue of migration to illustrate their strength, reliability and trustworthiness.

The responses to the perceived threat posed by migration take three key forms. The first is through a reinforcement of borders. As we show in Chapter Two, we are currently experiencing an unprecedented level of investment in border security. This includes physical borders – walls and fences made taller, deeper and more impenetrable – as well as their surveillance by military personnel and hardware. It also includes the role of technology, increasingly through biometrics. The second is through efforts to regulate mobility. Obviously, this happens through border reinforcement and security measures, making it more difficult for people to physically pass from one territory to another. However, it also takes place using legal mechanisms, such as formal migration schemes, discussed in more detail in Chapter Three. There has been a proliferation of legal migration routes in recent years, the terms of which change regularly. There is also a growing reliance on migration schemes that are designed as temporary from the outset, limiting the ability of people to develop a sense of formal belonging in their place of residence. This is the third response to the perceived threat of migration, which is discussed in more detail in Chapter Four. Here, we show how citizenship, as a marker of formal belonging, is becoming more difficult to attain for many migrants, whether because of cost or legal requirements. We also show how many migrants and some citizens, regardless of formal status, are marked as not belonging by virtue of race, ethnicity, religious beliefs or linguistic ability. As citizenship becomes more difficult to attain, and other forms of belonging are increasingly challenged, the result is that many residents of the UK and the US are living in a form of legal, political and social limbo.

One other outcome of these political upheavals has been the gradual edging towards the Right of mainstream political parties on issues of migration and citizenship. The rise of both right- and left-wing populism in the wake of the global financial crisis has destabilised the 'post-political' consensus and left mainstream political parties scrambling to appeal to a new, as-yet-undefined, voting constituency. The fierce electoral contestations between new nationalist and isolationist campaigns on the Right and the resurgence of social-democratic or radical Left campaigns is indicative of the era of political disruption. However, we also see more insidious manifestations of such political contests in the attempts by various political parties to position themselves to exploit the perception of popular xenophobia. Following Brexit in the UK, for example, the Conservatives outlined harder rhetoric regarding border control and limiting migration. However, Labour's Jeremy Corbyn was also pressured into supporting a 'tough on immigration' stance in an attempt to appease older Labour voters who had been swayed by the UK Independence Party (UKIP). As we have argued, these events should not be considered as a unified direction; rather, they are indicative of a loss of consensus. This is also indicated by the wider geopolitical impacts of Brexit and Trump. Leaders in neighbouring countries, such as Ireland's Leo Varadkar and Canada's Justin Trudeau, have sought to position themselves as a response, and in opposition, to Trump and Brexit divisions. However, rather than staking out more fundamentally progressive positions on the imbalanced global norms around migration and citizenship, these responses often seek to reassert the return to a 'late-liberal' status quo.

However, the story of migration and citizenship in the era of Trump and Brexit does not end here. Certainly, both the UK and US governments and other politicians are trying to restrict migration and citizenship rights, but their efforts are not absolute. As we show, these rights remain, or are enhanced, for small groups in the population. This is particularly the case for those who are ranked high on the hierarchy of acceptability, such as those with extensive personal wealth or in-demand skills. Mobility across borders, migrant status and, in the longer term, citizenship are enabled for this small category of people. In many ways, this reinforcement of privilege is an expected outcome of efforts to control migration and citizenship. What we have shown, though, is that these efforts may well have unintended, and unexpected, outcomes. Chapter Two charts the thorny problem of the border between Northern Ireland and the Republic of Ireland, and its likely status following Brexit. While advocates of Brexit emphasised taking back control of borders, it appears that they did not consider this particular border in any detail. Now, plans for control over the UK's borders are in abeyance because of the political difficulties in establishing a physical border between the UK and the EU on the island of Ireland. The US Travel Ban, discussed in detail in Chapter Three, also illustrates the counterproductive nature of efforts to control mobility. Courts have blocked the ban, or required it to be modified, in the process highlighting that there are limits to how a state might control mobility, and to the conditions under which it wishes to do so. When we discuss citizenship in Chapter Four, we show how Brexit has resulted in a rush of UK citizens applying for Irish, and consequently EU, citizenship. Irish ethnicity, previously viewed as suspicious, is now being translated into alternative forms of belonging as citizenship bleeds across borders.

Unintended consequences provide one form of disruption to attempts to regulate migration and citizenship. A second, powerful disruption is provided by those who actively organise to transgress borders, enable mobility or expand the practice of belonging. This includes activists in camps across Europe, such as the Calais 'Jungle' in north-eastern France. There, volunteers helped to support and organise asylum seekers and, in some instances, assisted them to travel to the UK. It includes activism along the Mexico–US border such as the work of No More Deaths, discussed in Chapter Two. Sanctuary cities, which have spread across the US, the UK and further, 'offer protection to illegalized migrants' (Bauder, 2017: 176), often in opposition to national-level policies and/or laws. There are also large-scale regularisation campaigns that seek to provide more legal certainty or even status for undocumented migrants. An example is the Deferred Action for Childhood Arrivals (DACA) programme, introduced by President Obama in 2012. This allowed undocumented migrants who had moved to the US as children to apply for permission to work, and prevented their deportation (Batalova et al, 2014). We take hope from these disruptions because they offer clear examples of alternative 'border thinking' (Mignolo, 2000). Rather than treating migrants as the scapegoats for broader societal changes and insecurities (Pred, 2000), these actions instead focus on people's shared humanity as they challenge efforts to restrict people's right to move and their ability to belong.

Thus, the current disruptions have transformed some of the policies, practices and norms relating to mobility and citizenship. However, perhaps more substantially, the visibility of these events has both opened a space for heightened forms of nationalism and exclusionary policies, and enabled the creation of new forms of political activism and subjectivity that seek to expand and recast what it means to move and to belong. In this moment of rupture, notions of borders, mobility and citizenship – which are always more precarious than they appear – are being reconfigured on a number of scales. Although these processes have led to some troubling events, we take hope from the difference that exists between transformations at the global or national level and the more complex and ambiguous reconfigurations of belonging, allegiance and citizenship that are taking place on the ground.

References

Adey, P. (2010) *Mobility*, Abingdon and New York, NY: Routledge.

Allegretti, A. (2016) 'Daily Mail corrects front page on "we're from Europe" smuggled migrants actually from Kuwait and Iraq', *Huffington Post*, 21 June. Available at: http://www.huffingtonpost.co.uk/entry/daily-mail-correction-were-from-europe-eu-referendum_uk_5763cfe6e4b01fb6586374d8

Anderson, B. (1983) *Imagined communities*, New York, NY: Verso.

Anderson, B. (2013) *Us & them: The dangerous politics of immigration control*, Oxford: Oxford University Press.

Anderson, N. (2017) '"Make no mistake, it's a hard border" – Varadkar rejects using the US Canadian border as a template for Ireland', *Irish Independent*, 22 August. Available at: http://www.independent.ie/irish-news/news/make-no-mistake-its-a-hard-border-varadkar-rejects-using-the-us-canadian-border-as-a-template-for-ireland-36059078.html

Aranda, E. and Vaquera, E. (2011) 'Unwelcomed immigrants: experiences with immigration officials and attachment to the United States', *Journal of Contemporary Criminal Justice*, 27(3): 299–321.

Arreola, D.D. (2005) 'Forget the Alamo: the border as place in John Sayles' *Lone star*', *Journal of Cultural Geography*, 23(1): 23–42.

Arreola, D.D. (2010) 'The Mexico–US borderlands through two decades', *Journal of Cultural Geography*, 27(3): 331–51.

Atkinson, R. (2016) 'Limited exposure: social concealment, mobility and engagement with public space by the super-rich in London', *Environment and Planning A*, 48(7): 1302–17.

Bagenstos, S. (2017) 'Disability, universalism, social rights, and citizenship', *Cardozo Law Review*, 39(2): 413–36.

Batalova, J., Hooker, S. and Capps, R. (2014) *DACA at the two-year mark: A national and state profile of youth eligible and applying for deferred action*, Washington, DC: Migration Policy Institute. Available at: https://www.migrationpolicy.org/research/daca-two-year-mark-national-and-state-profile-youth-eligible-and-applying-deferred-action

Bauder, H. (2017) 'Sanctuary cities: policies and practices in international perspective', *International Migration*, 55(2): 174–87.

BBC News (2017) 'Rise in hate crime in England and Wales', 17 October. Available at: http://www.bbc.com/news/uk-41648865

Berlant, L. (1997) *The queen of America goes to Washington City: essays on sex and citizenship*, Durham, NC: Duke University Press.

Bianchini, S. (2017) *Liquid nationalism and state partitions in Europe*, Cheltenham: Edward Elgar.

Bloomberg (2018) 'Everything we know about Donald Trump's proposed border wall', *Fortune*, 19 January. Available at: http://fortune.com/2018/01/19/donald-trump-border-wall/

Bourdieu, P. (1984) *Distinction: A social critique of the judgement of taste* (trans Nice, R.), Cambridge, MA: Harvard University Press.

Bowden, G. (2016) 'Calais child refugee media coverage "incredibly dangerous" charities say', *Huffington Post*, 21 October. Available at: http://www.huffingtonpost.co.uk/entry/calais-child-refugee-media-coverage-incredibly-dangerous-charities-say_uk_580a0231e4b056572d8265aa

Brown, M.P. (1995) *RePlacing citizenship: AIDS activism and radical democracy*, New York, NY: Guilford Press.

Brown, W. (2010) *Walled states, waning sovereignty*, New York, NY: Zone.

Brubaker, R. (2017) 'Populism's perfect storm', *Boston Review*, 11 July. Available at: http://bostonreview.net/politics/rogers-brubaker-populisms-perfect-storm

Butler, J. (2006) *Precarious life: The powers of mourning and violence*, London: Verso.

Butler, J. (2016) *Frames of war: When is life grievable?*, London: Verso Books.

Carmody, P. (2017) 'US–Russian geopolitics: the ghost in the machine and neoliberalism in one country', *Planetgeogblog*, 30 January. Available at: http://planetgeogblog.wordpress.com/2017/01/30/us-russian-geopolitics-the-ghost-in-the-machine-and-neoliberalism-in-one-country-by-padraig-carmody/

Casas-Cortes, M., Cobarrubias, S. and Pickles, J. (2015) 'Riding routes and itinerant borders: autonomy of migration and border externalization', *Antipode*, 47(4): 894–914.

Center for the Study of Hate and Extremism (2017) 'Final U.S. status report: hate crime analysis and forecast 2016/2017', California State University San Bernardino. Available at: https://csbs.csusb.edu/sites/csusb_csbs/files/Final%20Hate%20Crime%2017%20Status%20Report%20pdf.pdf

Central Statistics Office (2017a) 'Press statement Census 2016 results profile 6 – commuting in Ireland'. Available at: http://www.cso.ie/en/csolatestnews/pressreleases/2017pressreleases/pressstatementcensus2016resultsprofile6-commutinginireland/

Central Statistics Office (2017b) 'Table E7047 population usually resident and present in the state 2011 to 2016 by nationality, census year, birthplace and age group (2011–2016)'. Available at: http://www.cso.ie

Chu, B. (2017) 'If you think we need to "take back control" of our borders, you don't understand what that actually means', *The Independent*, 2 July. Available at: http://www.independent.co.uk/voices/brexit-customs-union-and-single-market-freedom-of-movement-immigration-border-control-what-does-it-a7819186.html

Cohen, C.J. (2010) *Democracy remixed: Black youth and the future of American politics*, New York, NY: Oxford University Press.

Coleman, M. (2007) 'Immigration geopolitics beyond the Mexico–US border', *Antipode*, 39(1): 54–76.

Coleman, M. (2012) 'Immigrant il-legality: geopolitical and legal borders in the US, 1882–present', *Geopolitics*, 17(2): 402–22.

Connelly, T. (2018) 'The Brexit veto: how and why Ireland raised the stakes', *RTE News*, 18 November. Available at: https://www.rte.ie/news/analysis-and-comment/2017/1117/920981-long-read-brexit/

Cooper, C. (2016a) 'EU referendum: Northern Ireland peace process could be set back by Brexit, says Lord Mandelson', *The Independent*, 15 March.

Cooper, C. (2016b) 'EU referendum: Tony Blair and John Major warn Brexit will "tear apart" Britain', *The Independent*, 9 June.

Countable (no date) 'A history of Trump's border wall'. Available at: http://www.countable.us/articles/418-history-trump-s-border-wall

Cresswell, T. (2010) 'Towards a politics of mobility', *Environment and Planning D: Society and Space*, 28: 17–31.

Crouch, C. (2004) *Post-democracy*, Cambridge: Polity.

Croucher, S. (2007) '"They love us here": American migrants in Mexico', *Dissent*, 54(1): 23–8.

Croucher, S. (2009) 'Migrants of privilege: the political transnationalism of Americans in Mexico', *Identities: Global Studies in Culture and Power*, 16(4): 463–91.

Crutsinger, M. (2018) 'Mulvaney says Trump budget will include money for Mexico border wall', *Chicago Tribune*, 11 February. Available at: http://www.chicagotribune.com/news/nationworld/politics/ct-trump-budget-border-wall-20180211-story.html

Dale, D. (2017) 'Trump's Homeland Security chief says he wants less restrictive Canadian border', *The Star*, 5 April. Available at: http://www.thestar.com/news/world/2017/04/05/trumps-homeland-security-chief-says-he-wants-less-restrictive-canadian-border.html

Daly, M. (2001) 'Irish nationality and citizenship since 1922', *Irish Historical Studies*, 32(127): 377–407.

Darling, J. (2009) 'Becoming bare life: asylum, hospitality, and the politics of encampment', *Environment and Planning D: Society and Space*, 27(4): 649–65.

Davies, T. and Isakjee, A. (2015) 'Geography, migration and abandonment in the Calais refugee camp', *Political Geography*, 49: 93–5.

DeBonis, M. (2018) 'House passes changes to Americans with Disabilities Act over activists' objections', *Washington Post*, 15 February.

Department of Foreign Affairs and Trade (2018) 'Passport and citizenship by descent applications from Northern Ireland and Great Britain in 2017', 1 January. Available at: https://dfa.ie/news-and-media/press-releases/press-release-archive/2018/january/passport-citizenship-figures-2017/

Devereaux, R. (2018) 'Nine humanitarian activists face federal charges after leaving water for migrants in the Arizona desert', *The Intercept*, 24 January. Available at: https://theintercept.com/2018/01/23/no-more-deaths-arizona-border-littering-charges-immigration/

European Commission (2017) 'Joint report from the negotiators of the European Union and the United Kingdom government on progress during phase 1 of negotiations under Article 50 on the United Kingdom's orderly withdrawal from the European Union', TF0 (2017) 19 – Commission to EU 27, 8 December. Available at: https://ec.europa.eu/commission/sites/beta-political/files/joint_report.pdf

European Commission (2018) 'European Commission draft withdrawal agreement on the withdrawal of the United Kingdom of Great Britain and Northern Ireland from the European Union and the European Atomic Energy Community', TF50 (2018) 33 – Commission to EU 27, 28 February. Available at: https://ec.europa.eu/commission/publications/draft-withdrawal-agreement-withdrawal-united-kingdom-great-britain-and-northern-ireland-european-union-and-european-atomic-energy-community_en

Faist, T. (2013) 'The mobility turn: a new paradigm for the social sciences?', *Ethnic and Racial Studies*, 36(11): 1637–46.

Friedman, T.L. (2006) *The world is flat: The globalized world in the twenty-first century*, London: Penguin.

Fukuyama, F. (2006) *The end of history and the last man*, New York, NY: Simon and Schuster.

Gaw, K. (2016) 'Northern Ireland's greatest fear from a Brexit is the return to conflict; ours is a hard-won peace, but it would be instantly jeopardised if Britain were to vote to leave the EU', *The Guardian*, 22 June.

Geier, B. (2015) 'Donald Trump wants to stop all Muslim immigration', *Fortune*, 7 December. Available at: http://fortune.com/2015/12/07/donald-trump-proposes-stopping-all-muslim-immigration/

Gieseking, J.J. (2016) 'Crossing over into neighbourhoods of the body: urban territories, borders and lesbian–queer bodies in New York City', *Area*, 48(3): 262–70.

Gilmartin, M. (2008) 'Migration, identity and belonging', *Geography Compass*, 2(6): 1837–52.

Gilmartin, M. (2015) *Ireland and migration in the twenty-first century*, Manchester: Manchester University Press.

Gilroy, P. (1991) *'There ain't no black in the Union Jack': The cultural politics of race and nation*, Chicago, IL: University of Chicago Press.

Glick Schiller, N. and Salazar, N.B. (2013) 'Regimes of mobility across the globe', *Journal of Ethnic and Migration Studies*, 39(2): 183–200.

Globe and Mail (2017a) 'Globe editorial: why Canada's border problems will only get worse under Donald Trump', *The Globe and Mail*, 7 August. Available at: http://beta.theglobeandmail.com/opinion/editorials/globe-editorial-why-canadas-border-problems-will-only-get-worse-under-donald-trump/article35896530/?ref=http://www.theglobeandmail.com&

Globe and Mail (2017b) 'Globe editorial: time to fix our uniquely Canadian border mess', *The Globe and Mail*, 16 August. Available at: http://beta.theglobeandmail.com/opinion/editorials/globe-editorial-time-to-fix-our-uniquely-canadian-border-mess/article36004741/?ref=http://www.theglobeandmail.com&

González, M.C. (2017) 'Women's group plans braids across border, March', *El Paso Times*, 12 January. Available at: http://www.elpasotimes.com/story/news/local/el-paso/2017/01/12/womens-group-plans-braids-across-border-march/96486180/

Goodwin, M. and Milazzo, C. (2017) 'Taking back control? Investigating the role of immigration in the 2016 vote for Brexit', *The British Journal of Politics and International Relations*, 19(3): 450–64.

HM Government (2017) 'Northern Ireland and Ireland position paper'. Available at: https://www.gov.uk/government/publications/northern-ireland-and-ireland-a-position-paper

Hufbauer, G.C. and Oegg, B. (2000) 'Targeted sanctions: a policy alternative', *Law and Policy in International Business*, 32: 11–21.

Irish Government (2017) 'Ireland and the negotiations on the UK's withdrawal from the European Union: the government's approach'. Available at: https://merrionstreet.ie/en/EU-UK/Key_Irish_Documents/Government_Approach_to_Brexit_Negotiations.pdf

Irish Independent (2016) 'Halt: why post-Brexit border posts could put a stop to business', *Irish Independent*, 27 February.

Isin, E.F. (2001) *Being political: Genealogies of citizenship*, Minneapolis, MN: University of Minnesota Press.

Isin, E.F. and Ruppert, E. (2015) *Being digital citizens*, London: Rowman & Littlefield.

Johnson, L. (2015) 'Material interventions on the US–Mexico border: investigating a sited politics of migrant solidarity', *Antipode*, 47(5): 1243–60.

Jones, R. (2016) *Violent borders: Refugees and the right to move*, London: Verso Books.

Jones, R. and Johnson, C. (2016) 'Border militarisation and the re-articulation of sovereignty', *Transactions of the Institute of British Geographers*, 41(2): 187–200.

Jordan, M. (2017) 'Citizenship applications in the U.S. surge as immigration talk toughens', *New York Times*, 27 October.

Kaye, L., Monzani, C., Silverstone, T. and Tait, M. (2017) 'British expats in Spain count the Costa Brexit', video, *The Guardian*, 16 March. Available at: https://www.theguardian.com/politics/video/2017/mar/16/british-expats-in-spain-count-the-costa-brexit-video

Kelly, F. (2017) 'US–Canada border would not work in Ireland, Varadkar says', *Irish Times*, 21 August. Available at: https://www.irishtimes.com/news/politics/us-canada-border-would-not-work-in-ireland-varadkar-says-1.3193744

Kelpie, C. (2016) 'Talks already under way to bring in electronic border with North', *Irish Independent*, 4 August.

Kennedy, M. (2017) 'Supreme Court Allows "grandparent" exemption to Trump travel ban', *NPR*, 19 July. Available at: http://www.npr.org/sections/thetwo-way/2017/07/19/538115295/supreme-court-upholds-grandparent-exemption-to-trump-travel-ban

Khoshneviss, H. (2017) 'Accountability in a state of liminality: Iranian students' experiences in American airports', *Mobilities*, 12(3): 311–23.

Kim, S. (2014) 'Britain tops list of world's most powerful passports', *The Telegraph*, 26 June. Available at: http://www.telegraph.co.uk/travel/news/Britain-tops-list-of-worlds-most-powerful-passports/

Knickmeyer, E. and Zoll, R. (2017) 'Despair, confusion reign as Trump's travel ban hits', *Associated Press*, 29 January.

Koh, S.Y. and Wissink, B. (2018) 'Enabling, structuring and creating elite transnational lifestyles: intermediaries of the super-rich and the elite mobilities industry', *Journal of Ethnic and Migration Studies*, 44(4): 592–609.

Krogstad, J.M., Passel, J.S. and Cohn, D. (2017) '5 facts about illegal immigration', Pew Research Centre, 27 April. Available at: http://www.pewresearch.org/fact-tank/2017/04/27/5-facts-about-illegal-immigration-in-the-u-s/

Kuttner, R. (2017) 'White nationalism and economic nationalism', *American Prospect*. Available at: http://prospect.org/article/white-nationalism-and-economic-nationalism

Laughland, O. (2017) 'Trump travel ban extended to blocks on North Korea, Venezuela and Chad', *The Guardian*, 25 September. Available at: https://www.theguardian.com/us-news/2017/sep/25/trump-travel-ban-extended-to-blocks-on-north-korea-and-venezuela

Layoun, M. (2001) *Wedded to the land? Gender, boundaries and nationalism in crisis*, Durham, NC: Duke University Press.

Lee, E. (2002) 'The Chinese exclusion example: race, immigration, and American gatekeeping, 1882–1924', *Journal of American Ethnic History*, 21(3): 36–62.

Lee, M.Y.H (2015) 'Donald Trump's false comments connecting Mexican immigrants and crime', *Washington Post*, 8 July. Available at: http://www.washingtonpost.com/news/fact-checker/wp/2015/07/08/donald-trumps-false-comments-connecting-mexican-immigrants-and-crime/?utm_term=.9d204ef42151

Longmore, P.K. (2003) *Why I burned my book and other essays on disability*, Philadelphia, PA: Temple University Press.

Léonard, S. (2010) 'EU border security and migration into the European Union: FRONTEX and securitisation through practices', *European Security*, 19(2): 231–54.

López, M.P. (2004) 'More than a license to drive: state restrictions on the use of driver's licenses by noncitizens', *Southern Illinois University Law Journal*, 29: 91–128.

Lorey, I. (2015) *State of insecurity: Government of the precarious*, London: Verso.

MacShane, D. (2017) *Brexit, no exit: why (in the end) Britain won't leave Europe*, London: I.B. Tauris.

Maidenberg, M. (2017) 'As travel industry awaits slowdown, travelers pack bags – for now', *New York Times*, 20 June.

McCarthy, T. and Laughland, O. (2017) 'Trump travel ban: Supreme Court allows enforcement as appeals proceed', *The Guardian*, 5 December.

McDonnell, F. (2016) 'North gripped by uncertainty over Brexit referendum; there are growing fears about what will happen if the UK votes to leave the EU', *Irish Times*, 7 June.

McDowell, L. (2009) 'Old and new European economic migrants: whiteness and managed migration policies', *Journal of Ethnic and Migration Studies*, 35(1): 19–36.

McGarry, J. and O'Leary, B. (2006a) 'Consociational theory, Northern Ireland's conflict, and its agreement. Part 1: what consociationalists can learn from Northern Ireland', *Government and Opposition*, 41(1): 43–63.

McGarry, J. and O'Leary, B. (2006b) 'Consociational theory, Northern Ireland's conflict, and its agreement. 2. What critics of consociation can learn from Northern Ireland', *Government and Opposition*, 41(2): 249–77.

McMurry, C. (2017) 'We'll work to avoid a hard border, says EU envoy as he sets sights on trip north', *Belfast Telegraph*, 12 May.

Mignolo, W. (2000) *Local histories/global designs: Coloniality, subaltern knowledges, and border thinking*, Princeton, NJ: Princeton University Press.

Migration Observatory (2017) 'EU migration to and from the UK', 30 August. Available at: http://www.migrationobservatory.ox.ac.uk/resources/briefings/eu-migration-to-and-from-the-uk/

Migration Policy Institute (2017) 'International migration statistics'. Available at: https://www.migrationpolicy.org/programs/data-hub/international-migration-statistics

Minca, C. and Rijke, A. (2017) 'Walls! Walls! Walls!', *Society and Space*. Available at: http://societyandspace.org/2017/04/18/walls-walls-walls/

Moriarty, G. (2017) 'British proposals "delusional", says SF', *Irish Times*, 17 August.

Morrow, D. and Byrne, J. (2016) 'Playing Jenga? Northern Ireland after Brexit', *Political Insight*, 7: 30–1.

Mould, O. (2017) 'The Calais Jungle: a slum of London's making', *City*, 21(3/4): 388–404.

Murray, S. (2017) 'What happened when British people were asked to draw the Irish border', *Journal.ie*, 29 November. Available at: http://www.thejournal.ie/brexit-ireland-border-2-3721935-Nov2017/

Murray, S. (2018) 'Explainer: why the "cast iron" guarantee for no hard Brexit border may now be in doubt', *Journal.ie*, 10 February. Available at: http://www.thejournal.ie/brexit-border-explainer-3844594-Feb2018/

Murtagh, P. (2017) 'Brexit fears prompt ex-British ambassador to become Irish citizen', *Irish Times*, 29 April.

National Travel and Tourism Office (2017) 'Monthly tourism statistics: US outbound travel by world regions 2015'. Available at: https://travel.trade.gov/research/monthly/departures/index.html

Naylor, L., Daigle, M., Zaragocin, S., Ramirez, M.M. and Gilmartin, M. (2018) 'Interventions: bringing the decolonial to political geography', *Political Geography*. Available at: https://doi.org/10.1016/j.polgeo.2017.11.002

New York Times (2016) 'Transcript of Donald Trump's immigration speech', 1 September. Available at: https://www.nytimes.com/2016/09/02/us/politics/transcript-trump-immigration-speech.html

O'Brien, S. (2017) 'EU's Brexit chief pledges soft border', *The Sunday Times*, 15 January.

O'Callaghan, C. (2011) 'The Queen in the postcolony. Ireland after Nama, 18 May'. Available at: https://irelandafternama.wordpress.com/2011/05/18/the-queen-in-the-postcolony/

O'Carroll, L. (2016) 'Ireland confident EU will keep Northern Irish border open post-Brexit; Country's ambassador to the UK says EU recognises region's "unique circumstances" and so would not create external border', *The Guardian*, 6 September.

OECD (Organisation for Economic Co-operation and Development) (2017) 'International migration database'. Available at: https://stats.oecd.org/Index.aspx?DataSetCode=MIG

Office for National Statistics (2017a) 'What information is there on British migrants living in Europe? Jan 2017'. Available at: https://www.ons.gov.uk/peoplepopulationandcommunity/populationandmigration/internationalmigration/articles/whatinformationisthereonbritishmigrantslivingineurope/jan2017

Office for National Statistics (2017b) 'Living abroad: dynamics of migration between the UK and Ireland'. Available at: https://www.ons.gov.uk/peoplepopulationandcommunity/populationandmigration/internationalmigration/articles/livingabroad/2017-09-21#how-many-people-who-were-born-in-ireland-are-living-in-the-uk

Office for National Statistics (2017c) 'Migration statistics quarterly report: November 2017'. Available at: https://www.ons.gov.uk/peoplepopulationandcommunity/populationandmigration/internationalmigration/bulletins/migrationstatisticsquarterlyreport/november2017

Office for National Statistics (2018) 'Overseas travel and tourism, quarterly'. Available at: https://www.ons.gov.uk/peoplepopulationandcommunity/leisureandtourism/datasets/overseastravelandtourism

Ong, A. (2006) 'Mutations in citizenship', *Theory, Culture, and Society*, 22(3): 499–503.

O'Toole, F. (2017) 'Brexiteers' foolishness gives Ireland control', *Irish Times*, 8 August. Available at: https://www.irishtimes.com/opinion/fintan-o-toole-brexiteers-foolishness-gives-ireland-control-1.3179299

Panetta, A. (2017) 'As U.S. shocks with NAFTA demands, other countries asking: what does Trump want?', *National Post*, 15 October. Available at: http://nationalpost.com/pmn/news-pmn/canada-news-pmn/as-u-s-shocks-with-nafta-demands-other-countries-asking-what-does-trump-want

Papademetriou, D. (2007) 'The age of mobility: how to get more out of migration in the 21st century', Migration Policy Institute. Available at: https://www.migrationpolicy.org/research/age-mobility-how-get-more-out-migration-21st-century

Peck, J. (2012) 'Austerity urbanism', *City*, 16(6): 626–55.

Povinelli, E.A. (2011) *Economies of abandonment: Social belonging and endurance in late liberalism*, Durham, NC: Duke University Press.

Pred, A. (2000) *Even in Sweden: Racisms, racialized spaces, and the popular geographical imagination*, Berkeley, CA, Los Angeles, CA, and London: University of California Press.

Price, M. and Breese, D. (2016) 'Unintended return: U.S. deportations and the fractious politics of mobility for Latinos', *Annals of the American Association of Geographers*, 106(2): 366–76.

Rancière, J. (1999) *Disagreement: Politics and philosophy*, Minnesota, MN: University of Minnesota Press.

Rankine, C. (2015) *Citizen: An American lyric*, Minneapolis, MN: Greywolf Press.

Rose-Redwood, C. and Rose-Redwood, R. (2017) 'Rethinking the politics of the international student experience in the age of Trump', *Journal of International Students*, 7(3): i–x.

Roszman, J (2017) 'How Brexit could unravel one of Bill Clinton's most historic achievements', *The Washington Post*, 10 July. Available at: http://www.washingtonpost.com/news/made-by-history/wp/2017/07/10/how-brexit-could-unravel-one-of-bill-clintons-most-historic-achievements/?utm_term=.bf8ee86e640e

Ryan, B. (2001) 'The Common Travel Area between Britain and Ireland', *The Modern Law Review*, 64(6): 855–74.

Ryan, B. (2016) 'The implications of UK withdrawal for immigration policy and nationality law: Irish aspects', ILPA EU Referendum Position Paper No. 8. Available at: http://www.ilpa.org.uk/resource/32154/eu-referendum-position-paper-8-the-implications-of-uk-withdrawal-for-immigration-policy-and-national

Sheller, M. (2016) 'Uneven mobility futures: a Foucauldian approach', *Mobilities*, 11(1): 15–31.

Sheller, M. and Urry, J. (2006) 'The new mobilities paradigm', *Environment and Planning A*, 38(2): 207–26.

Simpson, A. (2014) *Mohawk interruptus: Political life across the borders of settler states*, Durham, NC: Duke University Press.

Smith, L. (2018) 'Trump–Mexico border wall: what is happening, who will pay for it and what is the US president saying on the border barrier?', *The Independent*, 10 January. Available at: http://www.independent.co.uk/news/world/americas/us-politics/trump-mexico-wall-latest-updates-who-pay-what-us-president-border-barrier-say-prototypes-time-money-a8151681.html

Smith, M.P. (2001) *Transnational urbanism: Locating globalization*, London: Blackwell.

Somerville, H. (2017) 'Border wall prototypes a first small step on Trump campaign promise', *Reuters*, 24 October. Available at: http://www.reuters.com/article/us-usa-trump-wall/border-wall-prototypes-a-first-small-step-on-trump-campaign-promise-idUSKBN1CT007

Sparke, M.B. (2006) 'A neoliberal nexus: economy, security and the biopolitics of citizenship on the border', *Political Geography*, 25(2): 151–80.

Sparrow, A. (2018) 'Theresa May: Brexit will reduce access to single market – politics live'. Available at: https://www.theguardian.com/politics/blog/live/2018/mar/02/may-brexit-speech-theresa-may-to-use-her-brexit-speech-to-say-we-cant-have-everything-grayling-says-politics-live?page=with:block-5a9962dfe4b02f773c8d98bf#block-5a9962dfe4b02f773c8d98bf

Spence, E. (2014) 'Unraveling the politics of super-rich mobility: a study of crew and guest on board luxury yachts', *Mobilities*, 9(3): 401–13.

Squire, V. (2014) 'Desert "trash": posthumanism, border struggles, and humanitarian politics', *Political Geography*, 39: 11–21.

Sriskandarajah, D. and Drew, C. (2006) *Brits abroad: Mapping the scale and nature of British emigration*, London: Institute for Public Policy Research.

Staeheli, L.A., Ehrkamp, P. and Leitner, H. (2012) 'Dreaming the ordinary: daily life and the complex geographies of citizenship', *Progress in Human Geography*, 36(5): 628–44.

Stuesse, A. and Coleman, M. (2014) 'Automobility, immobility, altermobility: surviving and resisting the intensification of immigrant policing', *City & Society*, 26(1): 51–72.

Taylor, A. (2017) 'Refugees fleeing into Canada from the United States', *The Atlantic*, 16 February. Available at: http://www.theatlantic.com/photo/2017/02/refugees-fleeing-into-canada-from-the-us/516993/

Taylor, C. (2017) 'How activist artists on the US–Mexico border contest Donald Trump's wall', *The Conversation*, 24 July. Available at: http://theconversation.com/how-activist-artists-on-the-us-mexico-border-contest-donald-trumps-wall-79300

The White House (2017a) 'Executive order: border security and immigration enforcement improvements', 25 January. Available at: http://www.whitehouse.gov/the-press-office/2017/01/25/executive-order-border-security-and-immigration-enforcement-improvements

The White House (2017b) 'Executive order: protecting the nation from foreign terrorist entry into the United States', 27 January. Available at: https://www.whitehouse.gov/the-press-office/2017/01/27/executive-order-protecting-nation-foreign-terrorist-entry-united-states

The White House (2017c) 'President Trump and Prime Minister May's opening remarks', 27 January. Available at: https://www.whitehouse.gov/the-press-office/2017/01/27/president-trump-and-prime-minister-mays-opening-remarks

The White House (2018) 'President Donald J. Trump's State of the Union Address', 30 January. Available at: https://www.whitehouse.gov/briefings-statements/president-donald-j-trumps-state-union-address/

Till, K.E., Sundberg, J., Pullan, W., Psaltis, C., Makriyianni, C., Celal, R.Z., Samani, M.O. and Dowler, L. (2013) 'Interventions in the political geographies of walls', *Political Geography*, 33(1): 52–62.

Topinka, R.J. (2016) '"Wandering and settled tribes": biopolitics, citizenship, and the racialized migrant', *Citizenship Studies*, 20(3/4): 444–56.

Tuan, Y. (1977) *Space and place: The perspective of experience*, Minneapolis, MN: University of Minnesota Press.

UK Government (2017) 'Visas and immigration'. Available at: https://www.gov.uk/browse/visas-immigration

United Nations Statistics Division (2017) 'International migration: concepts and definitions'. Available at: https://unstats.un.org/unsd/demographic/sconcerns/migration/migrmethods.htm

US Department of State (2017) 'US visas'. Available at: https://travel.state.gov/content/visas/en/immigrate.html#special

US Travel Association (2016) 'U.S. travel and tourism overview (2016)'. Available at: https://www.ustravel.org/system/files/media_root/document/Research_Fact-Sheet_US-Travel-and-Tourism-Overview.pdf

US Travel Association (2017) 'US travel answer sheet'. Available at: https://www.ustravel.org/system/files/media_root/document/Research_Fact-Sheet_US-Travel-Answer-Sheet.pdf

Vollmer, B.A. (2017) 'Security or insecurity? Representations of the UK border in public and policy discourses', *Mobilities*, 12(3): 295–310.

White, A. and Gilmartin, M. (2008) 'Critical geographies of citizenship and belonging in Ireland', *Women's Studies International Forum*, 31: 390–9.

White, M. (2006) 'The dispositions of good citizenship: character, symbolic power and disinterest', *Journal of Civil Society*, 2(2): 111–22.

Wilkins, M. (2017) 'Asylum claimants processed in Canada', *Social Policy Trends*, August. Available at: https://www.policyschool.ca/wp-content/uploads/2017/08/Social-Policy-Trends-Asylum-Claimants-August.pdf

Wills, C. (2017) *Lovers and strangers: An immigrant history of post-war Britain*, London: Penguin Books.

Wise, J.M. (2000) 'Home: territory and identity', *Cultural Studies*, 14(2): 295–310.

Witsman, K. and Baugh, R. (2016) 'Annual flow report, U.S. naturalizations: 2015', US Department of Homeland Security, Office of Immigration Statistics, Policy Directorate. Available at: https://www.dhs.gov/sites/default/files/publications/Naturalizations_2015.pdf

Wood, P. and Young, J. (2016) 'A political ecology of home: attachment to place and political subjectivity', *Environment and Planning D: Society and Space*, 34(3): 474–91.

Wood, P. and Wortley, S. (2010) 'AlieNation: racism, injustice and other obstacles to full citizenship', CERIS, Ontario Metropolis Centre Working Paper Series, August.

World Tourism Organisation (2017) 'Tourism statistics'. Available at: http://www.e-unwto.org/toc/unwtotfb/current

Yuval-Davis, N. (1997) *Gender and nation*, London: Sage.

Zeffman, H. and Rogan, A. (2016) 'Bargaining begins for proxy border controls in Ireland', *The Times*, 11 October.

Zong, J. and Batalova, J. (2016) 'Naturalization trends in the United States', *Migration Information Source: The Online Journal of the Migration Policy Institute*, 10 August. Available at: http://www.migrationpolicy.org/article/naturalization-trends-united-states/

Zong, J., Batalova, J. and Hallock, J. (2018) 'Frequently requested statistics on immigrants and immigration in the United States'. Available at: https://www.migrationpolicy.org/article/frequently-requested-statistics-immigrants-and-immigration-united-states

Index